AA

touring
SCOTLAND

Produced by AA Publishing

Written by David Williams

Revised second edition 1996, published in this format 1998
First published 1992

Edited, designed and produced by AA Publishing.
© The Automobile Association 1998.
Maps © The Automobile Association 1998.

Distributed in the United Kingdom by AA Publishing, Norfolk House,
Priestley Road, Basingstoke, Hampshire
RG24 9NY.

A CIP catalogue record for this book is available from the British Library.

ISBN 0 7495 1658 5

Published by AA Publishing (a trading name of Automobile
Association Developments Limited, whose registered office
is Norfolk House, Priestley Road, Basingstoke, Hampshire
RG24 9NY. Registered number 1878835).

Colour separation: Daylight Colour Art, Singapore

Printed by G. Canale & C. S.P.A., Torino, Italy

Front cover: Eilean Donan Castle at sunset

CONTENTS

ABOUT THIS BOOK

This book is not only a practical guide for the independent traveller, but is also invaluable for those who would like to know more about the country.

The book is divided into 4 regions, each containing between 5 and 7 tours which start and finish in the towns and cities which we consider to be the best centres for exploration. Each tour has details of the most interesting places to visit en route. Panels cater for special interests follow some of the main entries – for those whose interest is in history, wildlife or walking, and those who have children. There are also panels which highlight scenic stretches of road and which give details of special events, gastronomic specialities, crafts and customs.

The simple route directions are accompanied by an easy-to-use map at the beginning of each tour, along with a chart showing how far it is from one town to the next in miles and kilometres. These can help you to decide where to take a break and stop overnight, for example. (All distances quoted are approximate.)

Before setting off it is advisable to check with the information centre at the start of the tour for recommendations on where to break your journey and for additional information on what to see and do, and when best to visit.

Entry Regulations

Passports are required by all visitors including citizens of EU countries. Visas are not required for entry into Britain by American citizens, nationals of the British Commonwealth and most European countries.

Customs Regulations

For goods bought outside the EU, you can import, duty free, 200 cigarettes or 100 cigarillos or 50 cigars or 250g of tobacco; one litre of alcohol over 22 per cent volume or 2 litres of alcohol not over 22 per cent volume or fortified or sparkling wine, plus 2 litres of still table wine; 60ml of perfume, 250ml of toilet water and £136 worth of other goods. If

Shaggy Highland cattle

goods are bought within the EU, you can import, duty paid, additional tobacco products, alcoholic drinks, gifts and other goods for personal use.

Emergency Telephone Numbers

Police, fire and ambulance tel: 999.

Health

Inoculations are not required for entry to Britain. Health insurance is recommended for non-EU citizens.

Currency

The unit of currency is the pound (£), divided into 100 pence (p). Coins are in denominations of 1, 2, 5, 10, 20 and 50 pence and one pound (£); Scottish notes are in denominations of £1, 5, 10, 20 and 50. Bank of England notes are also legal tender.

Credit Cards

All major credit cards are widely accepted throughout Scotland.

Banks

Banks are generally open between 9.30am and 5pm weekdays, though

times do vary from bank to bank and place to place. Some banks close for lunch.

Post Offices

Post offices generally open from 9am to 5.30pm Monday to Friday and 9am to noon on Saturdays. Times and days may vary from place to place.

Time

The official time is Greenwich Mean Time (GMT).

British Summer Time (BST) begins in late March when the clocks are put forward an hour. In late October, the clocks go back an hour to GMT. The official date is announced in the daily newspapers and is always at 2am on a Sunday.

Telephones

Insert coins after lifting the receiver; the dialling tone is a continuous tone.
Useful numbers:
Operator – 100
Directory Enquiries – 192
International Directory
Enquiries – 153
International Operator – 155
To make an international call, dial 00 (the international access code), then the country code, followed by the area code, omitting the first zero, then the local number.

Highland piper

SOUTHERN SCOTLAND

Southern Scotland is dominated by the grand mass of the Southern Uplands, the great band of hills which stretches right across the width of the country. For a long time it was easier to sail along the coastline than cross the hills, so the two coastal fringes were settled first. These narrow, fertile strips are still among the most populated parts of the region, with the best land devoted to cereals and herds of prime dairy cattle. Inland, the rolling uplands are home to the countless sheep which form the basis of the prosperous woollen and knitwear industries of the Borders.

The many castles and fortified houses found in the region are reminders of the centuries of border warfare that have shaped the history of the whole of southern Scotland. Cattle raiding, pillaging, looting and burning were commonplace, but perhaps the most poignant reminders of those turbulent days are the great Border abbeys of Melrose, Kelso, Jedburgh and Dryburgh which were mercilessly attacked and eventually destroyed by the English. Fortunately for us, their splendid ruins still survive to conjure up the past.

Boat showing the blue and white Ecosse flag in Eyemouth harbour

Today, the region is much more peaceful and most of today's 'invaders' come armed with a bucket and spade or a set of golf clubs. The eastern side of the country, with its beaches, seaside resorts, fishing villages and busy mill towns, has been a tourist area for some time, with many of its best-known places made famous by the region's best publicist, Sir Walter Scott. The west coast's literary figure, Robert Burns, is highly regarded as 'a man of the people', and his special place in the Scots' heart can be judged by the number of memorials, plaques and statues that mark his journeys through the country.

The region can never match the grandeur of the western Highlands or the great museums and palaces of central Scotland, but it does offer a relaxed way of life in an area imbued with tradition. Its people are proud of that fact. They are keen not to lose the unique flavour of their local culture and any visitor who witnesses a Border town's rugby match, will soon learn how independent the spirit is here.

The cycle museum at Drumlanrig Castle in Dumfries & Galloway

Tour 1

The journey along the Clyde coast is one of the finest in this part of Scotland, with glorious views over the Firth of Clyde to Arran and the smaller islands of the Clyde. With such views, it is no wonder that many Scots retire to this area. For the visitor, this scenery provides the backdrop to many places associated with Robert Burns, the national poet and the Scots' favourite literary figure.

Tour 2

Many visitors bypass this corner of the country, but there is a wealth of picturesque villages, historic buildings, sandy beaches and other attractions in this almost 'forgotten' land. The area is mainly agricultural and the great absence of industry and big towns has meant that many antiquities have been preserved and older building styles have survived. This is one of the warmest and driest parts of Scotland, factors that have helped foster agriculture – and palm trees!

Tour 3

The muddy creeks on the northern shore of the Solway Firth were havens to smugglers bringing contraband into Scotland. Given such a tradition, it comes as no surprise that the area's most famous figure was an exciseman – none other than Robert Burns, who spent his final years in the Dumfries area. The castles and granite towns of the coast contrast with large forests and rolling farmland inland.

Tour 4

Although the Clyde is normally thought of as an industrial river, the upper reaches are thronged with orchards and market gardens. Add a few castles and an impressive canyon and the Clyde Valley soon becomes one of the most surprising areas in this part of Scotland. The moors and hills above the valley are no less interesting and they have been home to Iron Age people, Romans and farmers – and weekend gold prospectors!

Tour 5

The tour follows many important river courses as they wind their way through the hills of the Southern Uplands, the land of the shepherd and the forester. Although the area's population has never been large, it has certainly seen many visitors. Some were unwelcome as they came to raid and plunder; others, the early tourists, came to sample the peaceful countryside and the delights of two of the country's most southerly spas.

Tour 6

The name of Sir Walter Scott is writ large in this area. He lived and worked here and also became one of Scotland's greatest novelists, to the extent that the Waverley novels gave their name both to a local railway line and to Edinburgh's main railway station. This is also the land of the ruins of the great Border abbeys, impressive medieval buildings that stand as monuments to man's craftsmanship – and powers of destruction.

Tour 7

The Border Country, of which this is part, has long seen the coming and going of armies and the number of castles found here is a measure of how dangerous an area this once was. Much of the coastline is rugged, and the cliff scenery quite spectacular, though in the north of the region the coastal scenery becomes gentler, giving way to fine beaches and grassy links that are ideal for golf. Inland, the rich agricultural district of the Merse supports many pretty villages, most of which nestle under the shelter of the Lammermuirs.

The Land
O' Burns

This tour starts in Ayr, once the chief port of western Scotland but now more famous for its associations with Robert Burns. And, indeed, throughout this tour the name of Scotland's most famous son keeps cropping up. . .

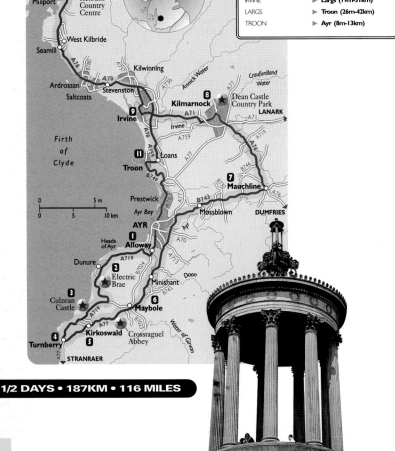

1/2 DAYS • 187KM • 116 MILES

▶ *Take the **B7024** from Ayr for 3 miles (5km) to the village of Alloway.*

❶ Alloway, Strathclyde
The Burns National Heritage Park was established here as this was where Robert Burns spent his early years. Burns was born in 1759 and he is regarded not only as Scotland's national poet but as one of her greatest literary figures. Although lionised by the predominantly Edinburgh-based literary celebrities of his day, he never abandoned his roots in the west and continued to work as a small farmer, and later as an exciseman. Like many great artists, he was never fully appreciated until well after his death, but now there are hundreds of Burns Societies all over the world, each year celebrating the poet's birthday (January 26) with such well-known favourites as *To a Haggis, Holy Willie's Prayer* and, probably his best-known work, *Auld Lang Syne*.

Opposite the Centre is the old ruined kirk where Burns' father is buried. This was a ruin even in Burns' day and it was here that Tam, in the poem Tam o' Shanter, saw warlocks, witches and Auld Nick (the devil). Also near by is the ancient and very beautiful Auld Brig o' Doon over which Tam escaped from the witches. Towering above the river is the Burns Monument which is set in a very pleasant park. Burns was born in the little thatched cottage known as Burns' Cottage. His father, William Burnes, built it around 1757 and it has been well preserved, not only as a memorial to the poet, but as a good example of local village architecture of the time. This type of

The Burns Monument and Brig O'Doon in Alloway

2-roomed cottage is known as a 'but and ben', with the kitchen in the front room and the living/bedroom room at the back ('ben'). The neighbouring museum holds a vast amount of Burns memorabilia.

▶ *Continue on the **B7024** for a short distance. Just after crossing the River Doon, turn right at an unclassified road to Doonfoot. Turn left when the coastal road (**A719**) is met, 8 miles (13km).*

❷ Electric Brae, Strathclyde
After the A719 passes Dunure and turns inland at Culzean Bay, the road goes 'up' the Electric Brae, a well-known and mind-boggling optical illusion. A car might appear to be travelling downhill, but drivers who come to a halt will find the car rolling backwards! On a pleasant summer afternoon, there is sometimes quite a queue of cars on this stretch of road trying to roll 'uphill'. Take care!

▶ *Continue on the **A719** for 5 miles (8km) to Culzean Castle.*

8 **Culzean Castle,**
Strathclyde

The present building is based on a medieval tower house that was later developed as a massive country house set within extensive parkland. It is now the National Trust for Scotland's major attraction and its country park has gardens, a nursery, a swan pond and a deer park. The information centre is housed in the attractive 18th-century buildings of Home Farm.

In the late 18th century, Robert Adam started work on remodelling the house. The interior decoration has since been painstakingly restored to his original designs to the extent that this is now the Scottish showpiece of Adam's work. The most outstanding features are the magnificent Oval Staircase and the Round Drawing Room.

i NTS, Culzean Castle

BACK TO NATURE

The coastline of Culzean has many different things to look for and is certainly worth exploring. You may find agates on the pebble beach and the rock pools have a wide variety of life in them including sea anemones, sea urchins and butterfish. During the summer there are many seabirds, while during the winter great northern divers might be seen offshore.

▶ *Continue southwards on the A719 for 5 miles (8km) to Turnberry.*

4 **Turnberry,** Strathclyde
This famous golfing centre is dominated by the Turnberry Hotel. The golf course sometimes plays host to the British Open.

The remains of the castle, which stands by the lighthouse, may have been the birthplace of Robert Bruce. In 1307 Bruce

was lured across the Clyde from Arran by a mystic fire and defeated the English force that was occupying the castle, destroying the buildings in the process.

▶ *Leave by the A77 and follow it northeast for 3 miles (5km) to Kirkoswald.*

5 **Kirkoswald,** Strathclyde
Kirkoswald has a number of connections with Robert Burns as his mother's family came from the village. Burns' characters of Tam and Kate from the poem *Tam o' Shanter* came from Kirkoswald and Souter

Culzean Castle, commanding a fine position above Culzean Bay

Johnnie's Cottage is on the main road. This thatched house of 1786 was the home of John Davidson, the local 'souter' (local term for shoemaker), and is now a museum furnished in the style of Burns' day. Burns would have attended the old Kirkoswald Church, now a picturesque ruin within a graveyard in which the poet's grandparents and great-grandparents are buried.

▶ *Continue on the A77 for 4 miles (6km) to Maybole.*

6 Maybole, Strathclyde
Many substantial buildings line
the narrow main street, the
most striking of which is
Maybole Castle, a 17th-century
castle. The castle is featured in
the ballad, *The Raggle Taggle
Gipsies*, in which the King of the
Gypsies, Johnnie Faa, persuad-
ed a Countess of Cassillis to
elope with him. Unfortunately
he was caught and hanged,
while the countess was imprisoned in the castle, in the room
with the little oriel window that
faces up High Street.

Maybole has a long history
and its oldest building is the
roofless Collegiate Church.
Most of the remaining parts,
although built in the 15th
century, are in the style is of the
13th and 14th centuries.

Crossraguel Abbey is met a
little before Maybole. This
relatively small Cluniac
monastery (it only had 10
monks in the 15th century) was
built in the mid-13th century. It
was very badly damaged in the
Wars of Independence
(1296–1357) and had to be
rebuilt. Although roofless, what
walls remain indicate the scale
of the establishment. The tall
tower house is a particularly
unusual building for an abbey.

The tower house of
Baltersan Tower lies between
the abbey and the village.

▶ *Continue on the **A77**, then
turn right at the **B743** to
Mauchline, 18 miles (29km).*

FOR HISTORY BUFFS

When driving along the road
neay Maybole, it is worth
remembering that the asphalt
or 'tarmacadam' surface was
named after a local man, John
Loudon MacAdam (1756–
1836). He experimented with
new ways of building roads by
using a layer of large stones
covered with layers of
sucessively smaller ones. His
ideas revolutionised road
building in this country.

7 Mauchline, Strathclyde
This little town is yet another in
the area which has a number of
associations with Robert Burns
as he lived at the farm of
Mossgiel, just north of
Mauchline. The most out-
standing building is the
National Burns Memorial; built
in 1896.

The church stands near the
centre of the town and in its
graveyard lie many people
associated with Burns, including
several of his children. Burns
featured some of them in his
poems, like the clockmaker
John Brown ('Clockie Brown' in
The Court of Equity), and a rogue
cattle dealer called McGavin
who was referred to as 'Master

Tootie, alias Laird McGaun' in
To Gavin Hamilton, Esq. By the
churchyard stands the Burns
House Museum where Burns
and his wife set up house in
1788; this also has a collection of
local material. It is open daily in
summer. Opposite the church
stands Poosie Nansie's Inn, the
setting for *The Jolly Beggars*.

$\boxed{i}$ *The Burns Memorial Tower,
Kilmarnock Road*

▶ *Leave by the **A76** and follow
it to Kilmarnock, entering the
town by the **A735**.*

Dominating the town: the National
Burns Memorial Tower at
Mauchline, built in 1896

8 Kilmarnock, Strathclyde
This industrial town, which is bigger than Ayr, built its affluence on the making of such diverse goods as whisky, carpets and various engineering products. Although much of the heart of the town has been changed by the building of modern shops, there are still some very fine buildings, many of them highly ornamented red or white sandstone structures, erected to reflect the wealth and aspirations of their builders.

The Dean Castle Country Park is on the northeast outskirts of the town. The attractive castle was a seat of the Boyds, lords of Kilmarnock, and was carefully restored in the 20th century. It houses a collection of arms, armour, tapestries and early musical instruments. The 200-acre grounds offer many opportunities for walks.

Kay Park, which is on the eastern side of the Craufurdland Water, has as its centrepiece the tall red sandstone Burns Monument which was erected in 1879. In 1786 Burns' first work was published and his Poems chiefly in the Scottish Dialect, usually known as the Kilmarnock Edition, brought him great fame – and the sum of £20.

FOR CHILDREN

The town's Galleon Centre offers many sporting facilities, including a crèche, a pool and an ice rink.
Five miles east of Kilmarnock, along the A71, Loudon Castle Country Park has Britain's largest roundabout.

---

i *62 Bank Street*

▶ *Leave by the **A759**. On reaching the **A71**, go to Irvine.*

9 Irvine, Strathclyde
Irvine has many attractions to its credit but the modern shopping centre, which crosses the River Irvine, dwarfs the older parts of the town and spoils Irvine's riverside location. The town prospered as a busy industrial centre and was Glasgow's main port before Port Glasgow was developed.

The wide-ranging Scottish Maritime Museum provides a fine introduction to local industrial and maritime history. Amongst the exhibits there are boats tied alongside the old harbour wall including a 'puffer' (a small cargo boat that served the west coast and its islands), the world's oldest remaining sea-coaster and a number of other craft, including lifeboats. The museum has exhibitions and displays of various shipbuilding crafts. The prize exhibit is the Victorian engine-shop from Stephen's Linthouse

The attractive exterior of Dean Castle – museum and country park

Boats alongside the harbour wall at Irvine's maritime museum

yard in Glasgow which has been re-erected here. This superb tall brick building is supported by the original cast-iron structure that was quite revolutionary when it was constructed in 1872. But industrial museums are not just about factories and their products, they are about the people who made this possible and the museum has restored a shipyard worker's 'room and kitchen' tenement house to what it would have looked like in 1910.

Harbour Street can be followed down to the river mouth where the Pilot House can be found. This was erected in 1906 with an automatic tide-signalling device which hoisted balls on top of the building to indicate the depth of the water.

The old part of the town on the other side of the river has

many interesting buildings to see. Robert Burns came here in 1781 to learn the trade of flax dressing (called 'heckling') and stayed at No 4 Glasgow Vennel, now a museum. He worked in a 'heckling shop' at No 10; 'hecklers' tended to be politically argumentative types, hence the modern useage of the word. Other places worth looking at

include the conservation area of Hill Street, the Townhouse and the Burns Club and Museum.

i New Street

▶ Leave by the **A737**, then join the **A78** (towards Greenock). Follow this to Largs.

10 Largs, Strathclyde
This popular seaside town has a long and attractive promenade giving fine views of the Firth of Clyde. Largs has a reassuringly prosperous air to it and many distinctive sandstone buildings, especially along its front. One unique structure that is hidden away and tends to be forgotten is the 1636 Skelmorlie Aisle, originally part of the parish church. Inside is an ornate Renaissance-style monument in the form of an archway which has a mass of fine detail carved in locally quarried sandstone. Above it is a painted ceiling

The round tower of Bowen Craig to the south of Largs, nicknamed The Pencil, commemorates the defeat of a Viking fleet here in 1263

which has survived remarkably well down the centuries. The burial ground also contains the burial vault of the local Brisbane family, one of whose members, Sir Thomas Brisbane, gave his name to the state's capital of Queensland, Australia.

At the southern end of the town, a walk along the coast leads to The Pencil, a tall monument that celebrates the Battle of Largs of 1263. A Viking fleet under King Haakon of Norway was driven ashore here and roundly defeated by the Scots led by Alexander III. This battle ended the Vikings' occupation of Scotland and in Largs' Vikingar Viking Heritage Centre there is a major exhibition celebrating Scotland's Viking heritage.

A regular car ferry crosses over to Great Cumbrae Island. The island's 'capital', Millport, has a pretty location looking over to Little Cumbrae Island and the beach is popular with families. Walking right round the island or across its top is a favourite outing and from the roadside Glaid Stone, at the summit of the island, there is a wonderful panorama over the Firth of Clyde.

i *Promenade, Largs; 28 Stuart Street, Millport (seasonal)*

SCENIC ROUTES

The journey along the Clyde Coast offers very fine views of the coast and the islands. On the southern part of the route, the view is dominated by the dome-shaped island of Ailsa Craig, often called 'Paddy's Milestone' as it lies halfway between Ireland and Clydeside. On the northern part of the route, the coastal road offers excellent views of the island of Arran.

▶ *Return south along the **A78** past Irvine, turning off right on the **A759** to Loans and Troon.*

⓫ Troon, Strathclyde

This is a pleasant seaside resort, with good beaches and renowned golf courses, one of which has hosted the British Open. The wide esplanade offers splendid views across the Firth towards Arran. Troon developed as a port in the 19th century in order to ship out coal from the Kilmarnock coalfield. The quayside wagons were initially hauled by horses but in 1816 a Stevenson steam locomotive was used, showing how the railways could be used to transform the country's transport system.

The inner harbour has now been turned into a marina and there is a good viewpoint near it on top of the Ballast Bank. This tall artificial mound was built up

Although usually yellowish in colour, Highland cattle are sometimes red or black

over a long time partly by ballast unloaded from coal boats returning from Ireland.

i *South Beach, Troon (seasonal)*

▶ *Leave by the **B749**. Turn right when the **A79** is met and follow this back to Ayr, 8 miles (13km).*

RECOMMENDED WALKS

The parks in Ayr, Culzean and Kilmarnock all offer level walking suitable for pushchairs and wheelchairs. There is also a large network of paths in Eglinton Park at Irvine and opportunities to see swans, roe deer and mink.

Galloway &
The Covenanters

2 DAYS • 255KM • 159 MILES Gentle scenery dominates this corner of the Scottish coast, while the mild weather ensures that plenty of people flock to its sandy beaches in the summer. Newton Stewart, the starting point on this tour, is a pleasant town on the River Cree, with few modern intrusions to spoil its charm.

The quayside at Wigtown, on the estuary of the River Bladnoch

[i] *Dashwood Square (seasonal)*

▶ *Leave by the **A714** and head southwards to Wigtown.*

❶ Wigtown, Dumfries and Galloway

This neat town has a main street wide enough to accommodate the local bowling green and a little park. This central area originally had a very practical use as it was where cattle were herded at night-time to prevent cattle thieves from taking them. At one end of the street are the imposing council offices (this was the county town of the former Wigtownshire) and at the other end is the site of the old mercat (market) cross. The museum is housed in the council offices.

A tall monument will be seen on entering the town. This commemorates the local Covenanters who were executed for their beliefs. The best-known local martyrs were Margaret Wilson and Margaret MacLachlan, who were executed by drowning in the River Bladnoch in 1685. The women's graves can be seen beside the parish church.

▶ *Continue on the **A714**, then turn left on to the **A746** to Whithorn, 11 miles (18km).*

2 Whithorn, Dumfries and Galloway

Whithorn has been a notable goal for travellers ever since pilgrims started to visit its important religious buildings. The religious settlement dates from the 5th century when St Ninian established a mission, and this is the site of the first recorded Christian Church in Scotland. Later, an important priory church was built but this was demolished during the Reformation and the prosperity of the village consequently declined.

Today, the old buildings are in ruins but a Romanesque doorway in what was the priory indicates the fine style of architecture in which they were built. Archaeologists have excavated the ground in front of the priory and have uncovered valuable evidence of the buildings that stood here. They have also unearthed hundreds of skeletons as they dug down through the ancient cemetery. These skeletons have provided fascinating clues to the life, health and death of the local people. The continuing investigations, known as the Whithorn Dig, have unearthed many interesting artefacts and these are now on display at the site's Discovery Centre, which is certainly worth a visit.

☐ *The Whithorn Dig (seasonal)*

▶ *Leave on the A746, then bear left at the B7004. Follow this to the Isle of Whithorn.*

3 Isle of Whithorn, Dumfries and Galloway

This picturesquely sited village is not in fact an island at all but does have a well-sheltered harbour which is frequented by fishing boats and many pleasure craft.

Just beyond the harbour is a grassy promontory with a lookout tower, and on a fine day Ireland, the Isle of Man, England and possibly even the hills of Wales can be seen. On the seaward side of the village stands the remains of St Ninian's Chapel, a 14th-century church.

▶ *Return along the B7004, bear left along a minor road, then follow the A747 to Monreith, 9 miles (14km).*

SCENIC ROUTES

The coastal roads near the Isle of Whithorn and from Monreith to Glenluce have extensive views over the Solway Firth and the northern reaches of the Irish Sea. Keep binoculars handy in order to see the English and Irish coasts and the Isle of Man.

---

4 Monreith, Dumfries and Galloway

Just before the village is reached, a road (left) to the St Medan Golf Club leads to a memorial to Gavin Maxwell (1914–69). This is in the form of a bronze otter – Maxwell was a writer and naturalist whose book about otters, *Ring of Bright Water*, was made into a film. A prehistoric spiral 'cup and ring' mark is plainly visible just below the memorial.

▶ *Continue on the A747, then turn left at the A75 (then right at the A747) to reach Glenluce, 16 miles (26km) away.*

FOR CHILDREN

Lower Knock Waterfowl Open Farm is on the A747 before Monreith and as well as waterfowl, it has goats, Shetland ponies, pot-bellied pigs and peacocks. It also has a children's play area and a campsite.

The picturesque harbour of the Isle of Whithorn

The remains of 12th-century Cistercian Glenluce Abbey

which has part of the original tiled floor still extant. One of the abbey's interesting architectural details that might be overlooked is the survival of the water-supply system which still has the original jointed earthenware pipes and lidded junction boxes.

▶ *Rejoin the **A75** and head towards Stranraer. Bear left at the **B7084**, then follow the **A716** towards Drummore. Turn right at the **B7065** to reach Port Logan.*

6 **Port Logan,** Dumfries and Galloway

Port Logan is a planned village originally laid out in 1818, with a little pier that has an attractive lighthouse at its end. On the other side of Port Logan Bay, a small cluster of buildings marks the location of the Logan Fish Pond, one of the most surprising places to be found in this corner of the country. This is a natural rock pool some 30 feet (9m) deep and 53 feet (16m) in diameter which holds mainly cod and pollack. It was established in 1800 as a fresh seawater 'larder' for nearby Logan House but is now a tourist attraction that will fascinate visitors especially as the fish will take food from the keeper's hand. Logan Botanic Garden lies beyond Port Logan Bay. This is an outstation of the Royal Botanic Gardens of Edinburgh and it has a marvellous collection of plants, especially in the well-sheltered walled garden.

5 **Glenluce,** Dumfries and Galloway

The village, developed as a staging post on the busy Stranraer to Carlisle road, is now a pleasant centre for exploring this corner of the southwest. As if to testify to the village's links with different types of transport, the motor museum has vintage cars and motorcycles amongst its exhibits.

Glenluce Abbey, to the northwest of the village, is an impressive ruined Cistercian monastery that was founded around 1190. Its best-preserved structure is the chapter house

The warm Gulf Stream keeps the local climate exceptionally mild so many exotic plants such as tree ferns and palms are able to flourish here.

▶ *Return along the **B7065** and **A716** to Sandhead, then turn left at the **B7042**. Turn left at the **A77** to reach Portpatrick.*

Ferry departing for Ireland from Stranraer harbour

---

7 **Portpatrick,** Dumfries and Galloway

One of the most attractive of Scotland's small seaside resorts, Portpatrick has a well-sheltered harbour ringed by colourful stone-built houses and hotels. Portpatrick is the nearest Scottish harbour to Ireland and it was once an important base for ferries, fishing boats and troop ships, but today it is mainly pleasure boats that tie up in the harbour.

Although the village is far from the Galloway Hills, many walkers arrive here as this is the start of the Southern Upland Way, a long-distance walk of over 200 miles (320km) that stretches right across southern Scotland and ends at Cockburnspath near Dunbar. The Way begins at the back of the harbour.

The ruins of Old Portpatrick Parish Kirk stand behind the seafront houses and its most notable feature is its four-storey circular tower. This was probably both a belfry and a beacon for the harbour. Steps from the seafront lead southward to the 16th-century Dunksey Castle. This was built around 1510 but was a ruin less than two centuries later. The walk to the castle gives splendid views of the coastline, especially if the day is fine.

▶ *Return along the **A77** and follow it for 9 miles (14km) to Stranraer.*

8 **Stranraer,** Dumfries and Galloway

Stranraer is the centre for shopping and services in this part of the country, and is also part of an important transport centre. It has a rail link direct to Glasgow, and a busy ferry service to Belfast and Larne in Ireland. Near the ferry terminal stands the North West Castle Hotel, the former home of Sir John Ross who gained fame exploring the Arctic in search of the Northwest Passage, the sea route north of Canada. Displays on his exploits are contained in the museum which also has exhibitions on the history and

FOR HISTORY BUFFS

Castle Kennedy stands beside the village of the same name, east of Stranraer. It was built by the 5th Earl of Cassillis, a Kennedy, whose family in the 15th and 16th centuries was very powerful in this part of Scotland. Burnt down in 1716, the gaunt ivy-clad tower is surrounded by pleasant gardans, laid out by William Adam, in which there is a fine collection of rhododendrons and azaleas.

BACK TO NATURE

South of Bargrennan, a road goes left to the Wood of Cree Nature Reserve which is under the care of the RSPB. The Wood of Cree is one of southern Scotland's best broadleaved woodlands and is sited by the marshy River Cree. Numerous birds may be seen, including the great spotted woodpecker and the tawny owl in the woods; snipe and water rail in the marshes; and tree pipit and redstart in the scrubland. The reserve has two marked walks: a woodland trail and a scrubland trail.

agriculture of the area. Stranraer's main antiquity is the Castle of St John which is right in the centre of town. This dates back to 1510 and was later used by the council as a gaol. Its rooftop exercise yard gives a fine view of the local scenery.

☐ *Bridge Street (seasonal)*

The wide, open beach of Girvan, with views to Ailsa Craig

▶ *Continue on the **A77** to Girvan.*

9 Girvan, Strathclyde
Girvan is a little seaside town whose pretty, sandy beach is popular with families during the summer. It has a busy harbour which is home to a number of fishing boats and some fishermen hire out their craft for fishing trips. This is probably the best place from which to view the rugged island of Ailsa Craig. The island is made from a fine-grained granite which was quarried for the making of high-quality curling stones. The island has a massive colony of gannets with over 10,000 pairs breeding there during the summer. Girvan's McKechnie Institute features exhibitions on the town and Ailsa Craig.

☐ *Bridge Street (seasonal)*

▶ *Leave by the **A714** and at Bargrennan turn left on to the unclassified road to Loch Trool.*

10 Loch Trool, Dumfries and Galloway
The loch sits within the Galloway Forest Park, a popular recreational area with nature trails that attract walkers, campers and sightseers.

▶ *Return along the unclassified road to Bargrennan, then turn left on to the **A714** to return to Newton Stewart.*

Queen of
the South

Dumfries' attractive setting on the banks of the River Nith has earned it the title 'Queen of the South'. This is the region's main town and its fine public buildings reflect the history and prosperity of the area. Inland from the 'granite towns' along this coast is a landscape dominated by farms and forests.

1/2 DAYS • 193KM • 118 MILES

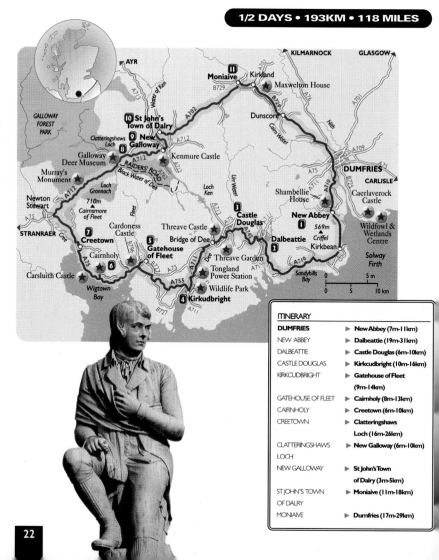

ITINERARY		
DUMFRIES	▶	**New Abbey (7m-11km)**
NEW ABBEY	▶	**Dalbeattie (19m-31km)**
DALBEATTIE	▶	**Castle Douglas (6m-10km)**
CASTLE DOUGLAS	▶	**Kirkcudbright (10m-16km)**
KIRKCUDBRIGHT	▶	**Gatehouse of Fleet (9m-14km)**
GATEHOUSE OF FLEET	▶	**Cairnholy (8m-13km)**
CAIRNHOLY	▶	**Creetown (6m-10km)**
CREETOWN	▶	**Clatteringshaws Loch (16m-26km)**
CLATTERINGSHAWS LOCH	▶	**New Galloway (6m-10km)**
NEW GALLOWAY	▶	**St John's Town of Dalry (3m-5km)**
ST JOHN'S TOWN OF DALRY	▶	**Moniaive (11m-18km)**
MONIAIVE	▶	**Dumfries (17m-29km)**

---

i **Whitesands**

▶ Leave by the **A710** (the
Solway Coast Road) and
follow it for 7 miles (11km)
to New Abbey.

BACK TO NATURE

The Wildfowl and Wetlands
Centre at Caerlaverock, southeast of Dumfries, is managed
to provide ideal feeding for
thousands of birds that come
here during the migrating season and the remainder of the
year. Over 12,000 barnacle
geese, plus many other
birds such as pink-footed and
greylag geese, whooper and
Bewick's swans and various
species of ducks are regular
visitors. The centre's hides
and observation tower are
located at Eastpark farm,
which is reached from the
B725.

FOR HISTORY BUFFS

Caerlaverock Castle was started in the 13th century and is
the most important castle in
the area. Unusually, it is
triangular in shape and is protected by a double-towered
gatehouse and a water-filled
moat. Both the Scots and the
English had a hand in reducing
the walls, but substantial parts
of the castle remain and there
are some nice interior
buildings.

❶ New Abbey, Dumfries
and Galloway
The village is best-known for
the ruins of Sweetheart Abbey,
or New Abbey, founded in the
13th century as a Cistercian
establishment. It is regarded as
one of Scotland's most beautiful
monastic ruins and, although
roofless, it still has massive walls

The Old Bridge over the Nith at
Dumfries, built by Dervorguilla,
foundress of Sweetheart Abbey

and a fine rose window. The
abbey was founded by
Dervorguilla, wife of John
Balliol, whose son became king
of Scotland in 1292. After her
husband died, Dervorguilla
carried his embalmed heart
around with her until she died
some 22 years later! She and the
heart were buried in front of the
high altar – hence the name of
the abbey. Dervorguilla also
founded Balliol College in
Oxford and named it after her
husband.

The 18th-century corn mill
in the village has been restored
to working order and is open to
the public. It is one of the finest
mills of its type in Scotland. Just
outside the village is
Shambellie House, where the
National Museum of Scotland
has a museum of costume.

▶ *Continue on the **A710** for 19
miles (31km) to Dalbeattie.*

2 Dalbeattie, Dumfries and
Galloway
Dalbeattie was established to
exploit the local granite which
was quarried at the nearby
Craignair quarry. Many of the
town's buildings are made from
this bright grey stone which
sparkles in the sunlight. While
some of the stone was used
locally, great quantities of it
were exported to construct such
buildings as London's Bank of
England, Liverpool's Mersey
Docks, the Eddystone
Lighthouse off Plymouth and
the Grand Harbour at Valetta, on
Malta. Dalbeattie makes a good
base for further exploring the
coastline.

⚏ *Town Hall (seasonal)*

Threave Castle, famous for its
impressive displays of flowers in all
seasons

▶ *Leave by the **A711**, then turn
right at the **A745** to Castle
Douglas, 6 miles (10km).*

3 Castle Douglas,
Dumfries and Galloway
The town was originally called
Carlingwark after the local loch,
but was renamed in 1792 by a
Sir William Douglas after he
had acquired the land. Castle
Douglas was then developed
into an important market town
and its horse and cattle fairs
helped attract the wealth that
built the spaciously laid-out
town centre. It now has plenty
of shops to make strolling
worthwhile.
   The NTS's extensive
Threave Garden is on the
outskirts and it is particularly
well known for its spring
displays of nearly 200 varieties
of daffodils. Threave Castle
stands on an islet in the River
Dee. Its four-storey tower was
built in the 14th century and it
is surrounded by an outer wall
of about a century later. One
rather unusual feature is that it
has a near complete medieval
riverside harbour.

⚏ *Markethill, Castle Douglas;
Threave Gardens (both
seasonal)*

▶ *Leave by the **B736** and turn
left when the **A75** is met.
Turn left at the **A711** and
follow this to Kirkcudbright.*

4 Kirkcudbright, Dumfries
and Galloway
Kirkcudbright's broad and
spacious streets are a delight to
stroll along as many old public
buildings, such as the 17th-
century Tolbooth, still stand.
The mercat (market) cross of
1610 is on the Tolbooth steps.
MacLellan's Castle, built in the
late 16th century, stands near
the harbour and dominates this
part of the town.
   The town has had a long
and colourful history, including
many connections with sea trading and piracy. In the late 16th
century the pirate Leonard
Robertson captured an English
merchant vessel and sold its
cargo to local lairds. When
Queen Elizabeth of England
complained to King James VI
he promised to investigate the

i Harbour Square (seasonal)

▶ Leave by the **A755** and turn left at the **A75**. Turn right at the **B796** to reach Gatehouse of Fleet.

5 Gatehouse of Fleet, Dumfries and Galloway
This was once a prosperous spinning and weaving village but it is now quiet and rather peaceful. There are numerous hotels, one of which, The Murray Arms, was where Robert Burns wrote *Scots Wha Hae.*

Cardoness Castle is just outside the village. This was built in the 15th century by the McCullochs and stands in a prominent position overlooking the Water of Fleet.

i Car Park (seasonal)

▶ Return along the **B796** and turn right at the **A75**. Follow this towards Creetown. Turn right at a narrow signposted road to Cairnholy, 8 miles (13km).

6 Cairnholy, Dumfries and Galloway
There are two monuments at Cairnholy. These were used

MacLellan's Castle, an impressive 16th century building which dominates Kirkcudbright

matter, which he did by appointing a commission manned by the very lairds who had bought the stolen goods. Such was justice!

The Stewartry Museum has a good collection of local material and a section on John Paul Jones. He joined the Union navy and fought against the British during the American War of Independence; his daring exploits included attacks on the British coast. During a 'quiet' time he had the audacity to visit this area in secret. Broughton House, in High Street, was the home of E A Hornel and is run by the NTS as a museum dedicated to the artist, who died in 1933.

Tongland Hydroelectric Power Station stands on the River Dee, to the north of Kirkcudbright. This is just one of the power stations in the Galloway Hydroelectric Scheme and there are organised tours around the buildings. Downstream of the station is the attractive Tongland Bridge built by Thomas Telford in 1805.

well over 3,000 years ago as burial sites and for ceremonies of some kind. Cairnholy I is particularly impressive, with its pillared façade and two tombs. The tombs would have originally been covered by a massive cairn of boulders but these were later removed, probably by farmers seeking easily obtained building stones.

▶ *Return to the **A75** and turn right. Leave the **A75** on the right at the signposted road to Creetown.*

◪ **Creetown,** Dumfries and Galloway
Creetown is another 'granite town' with many of its buildings made of the local grey stone. The Gem Rock Museum is sited in a former school and has a marvellous collection of minerals, fossils and many other exhibits from all over the world. Carsluith Castle will be seen on the left before entering Creetown. This started off as a rectangular tower in the 15th century but later additions gave it an L-shape and a balcony. It fell into ruins after 1748.

Prehistoric chambered tomb at Cairnholy I

▶ *Rejoin the **A75** and turn right. Turn right at the **A712** to the Clatteringshaws Forest Wildlife Centre near Clatteringshaws Loch (Galloway Forest Park).*

⓼ **Clatteringshaws Loch,** Dumfries and Galloway
This artificial loch is surrounded by moorlands and conifers and is within the boundary of the Galloway Forest Park. The park is home to many animals and there are herds of wild goat and deer on the southern shore of the loch. The Forest Wildlife Centre has lots of information on the wildlife, geology and history of the area and close by it is a reconstructed Romano-British hut from around AD 200–300, which is worth a look.

RECOMMENDED WALKS

There are a great number of walks in the Galloway Forest Park, including forest strolls and more strenuous walks on to the rugged hills.
Criffel (1,867 feet/569m), southwest of New Abbey, is the highest of the coastal hills. It offers tremendous panoramic views over the Solway Firth towards the Lake District.

Close to the Loch is Bruce's Stone, a memorial to Robert the Bruce, the Scottish King who, so legent says, learned a lesson in persistence from a spider. This overlooks the place where, in 1307, a small group of Scots defeated a force of English soldiers by starting a landslide which buried them.

Near the museum, the Raiders' Road goes off to the right through the forest and follows an old cattle rustlers' route. Different breeds of deer may be seen here and you may be lucky enough to see otters; buzzards, sparrowhawks and ravens can also be spotted on occasion.

▶ *Continue on the A712 for 6 miles (10km) to New Galloway.*

9 New Galloway, Dumfries and Galloway

This quiet little village stands above the Water of Ken. South of it stand the ruins of 16th-century Kenmure Castle which used to be an imposing house until partly dismantled in the 1950s.

▶ *Leave by the A712, then turn left at the A713 to reach St John's Town of Dalry, 3 miles (5km).*

10 St John's Town of Dalry, Dumfries and Galloway

The main street in this pleasant village is lined with white-washed cottages, at the top of which can be seen a peculiar little stone seat known as St John the Baptist's Chair. There is no evidence that he ever sat

The Robert Bruce memorial by the shores of Loch Trool in the Galloway Forest Park

upon it, but one of Sir Walter Scott's acquaintances found the legend intriguing enough to try and take it away. The Southern Upland Way follows the main street and passes the chair on its long coast-to-coast journey between Portpatrick and Cockburnspath. The church, which was erected in 1831, has several interesting gravestones. The most notable gravestone is the horizontal Covenanters' stone (to the Auchencloy Martyrs) in the corner of the churchyard, inscribed with the story of their shooting by Claverhouse.

▶ *Leave by the A702 and follow it for 11 miles (18km) to Moniaive.*

11 Moniaive, Dumfries and Galloway

Moniaive is best remembered for being the birthplace of James Renwick, the last Covenanter, who was hanged in Edinburgh. A monument to him has been erected at the edge of the village.

To the east, beyond Kirkland, stands Maxwelton House, the birthplace and home of Annie Laurie, about whom a famous ballad was composed. The original song was written around 1700, although a later version was penned in 1835. The house was built on to a 14th-century castle and houses a small museum of local lore and history.

▶ *Continue on to the A702, then turn right at the B729. Turn right at the A76 to return to Dumfries.*

1/2 DAYS • 190KM • 119 MILES

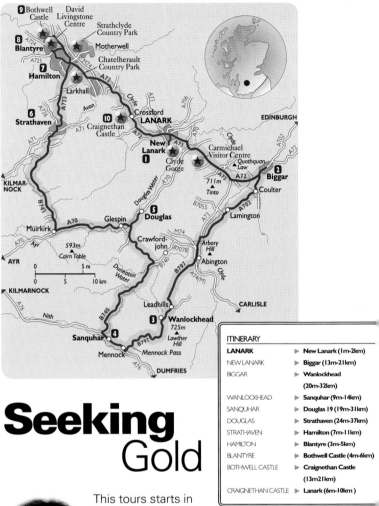

Seeking
Gold

This tours starts in Lanark, home to another Scottish hero, William Wallace, who is thought to have lived in nearby Castlegate before being caught up in the struggle against the English. A statue of him now stands above the door of the 18th-century church of St Nicholas. Lanark makes a good base from which to explore the surrounding hills and valleys of the Clyde Valley.

i Horsemarket, Ladyacre Road

▶ *Follow the local signs from the market for 1 mile (2km) to the village of New Lanark.*

RECOMMENDED WALKS

From New Lanark, it is possible to walk up the Clyde Gorge to the dam at the waterfall of Bonnington Linn. This magnificent gorge, formed about 12,000 years ago after the last Ice Age, has a number of fine waterfalls, notably Corra Linn. The water is used to power a hydroelectric power station, but on certain holiday weekends the station is closed down and the falls are at their most impressive.

❶ New Lanark, Strathclyde
The village is set in the magnificent wooded gorge of the River Clyde and within walking distance of Lanark itself. During the 18th century Richard Arkwright and David Dale visited the site and soon began establishing cotton mills here, with water power provided from Dundaff Linn, one of the smallest of the Falls of Clyde. At the beginning of the 19th century, Dale's son-in-law Robert Owen developed what was then the country's biggest cotton mill, employing over 2,000 people in the village, into a superb example of how an industrial undertaking could benefit the local people. The buildings were well constructed and spacious (for that time) and he took on pauper apprentices and housed and educated them. He also built the quaintly named Institute for the Formation of Character. Many of his ideas, including his refusal to use child labour, were revolutionary; what was even more astounding to other mill owners was that his ideas worked and his mills were well-run, efficient and profitable.
    Owen's bold experiments

The dramatically situated Falls of Clyde, well worth a walk from New Lanark

are celebrated in the visitor's facilities that occupy some of the old mill buildings. There are fascinating tales of what life was like in the mills and insights into how the Lowland and Highland Scots adapted to the arrival of the industrial age.

▶ *Return to Lanark, then leave by the A73. Turn left at the A72 and the A702 and follow this to Biggar, 13 miles (21km).*

FOR CHILDREN

The Discover Carmichael Visitor Centre lies between Lanark and Biggar. As well as numerous animals, there is also a collection of wax models of historical Scots figures.

Biggar Little Theatre has a complete Victorian theatre in miniature which is used for puppet plays. There is also a puppet exhibition and a chance to try your hand at outdoor Victorian games.

FOR HISTORY BUFFS

Iron Age people built a number of hillforts overlooking the Clyde Valley and these often have ramparts and ditches that were used as defensive structures. The locations were chosen for their lofty positions as there are good views from them. Notable ones include Arbory Hill (east of Abington) and Quothquan Law (west of Biggar).

2 Biggar, Strathclyde

Biggar's main street is even wider than Lanark's, a fact that may have encouraged the saying 'London's London, but Biggar's Biggar!'

For such a compact place, Biggar has a remarkable number of interesting places to visit. The oldest is Boghall Castle, now a ruin but once a substantial fortification that was besieged by both Regent Moray and Oliver Cromwell. The most unusual building in the village houses the Biggar Gasworks Museum, the oldest surviving rural gasworks in the country, built in 1839.

The Gladstone Court Museum (off High Street) contains a number of replica shops, a schoolroom, a bank and a post office, scenes which portray life in Victorian Biggar. Further down the street can be seen the small footbridge called the Cadgers Brig. Legend has it

that William Wallace crossed this in 1297 disguised as a cadger (a pedlar) to spy on the English army that was camped near by.

On one of the higher parts of the village stands St Mary's Church, founded in 1546, as the last pre-Reformation church in

SCENIC ROUTES

The route after Abington climbs through moorland into the Lowther Hills and after Wanlockhead the road descends to meet Nithsdale; this latter part, through the Mennock Pass, can be very beautiful in late summer when the heather and bracken are changing colour.

Scotland's oldest surviving rural gasworks houses the Biggar Gasworks Museum

Scotland. Opposite this is the Moat Park Heritage Centre, which has displays covering 6,000 years of history in Clydesdale. Behind it lies a small valley in which runs the Biggar Burn and this can be followed upstream to Greenhill, a farm that was relocated here, stone by stone, from

Wanlockhead lead mine – once a major mining centre but now closed down, although it's possible to take a tour of Loch Nell Mine

south of Tinto. This is a Covenanting museum, with relics and mementoes of the 17th century.

i 155 High Street (seasonal)

▶ Leave by the **A702** and follow this to Abington. Turn off at the **B797** which leads to Wanlockhead, 20 miles (32km).

3 Wanlockhead, Dumfries and Galloway

Sitting at an altitude of 1,533 feet (467m), this is Scotland's highest village. With neighbouring Leadhills, Wanlockhead was once a major lead mining centre, hence all the piles of debris that have been left here. Lead was probably mined here in Roman times, but the modern history of the mines started about 1675 and the industry managed to keep going until the 1950s. Gold has also been excavated in the area; the largest piece found was nearly 7oz (200g) in weight and is now in the British Museum.

Goldpanners sometimes come to the district to try their luck and skill in winning a few flakes from the streams.

A number of buildings associated with the mines, complete with mining equipment, have been preserved and these include the Pates Knowes Smelt Mine and the Wanlockhead Beam Engine. Guided tours into the Loch Nell Mine are available and the history of the mines and of the district is told in the village's Museum of Scottish Leadmining.

i   *Welcome Break Service Area, A74 northbound, Abington*

RECOMMENDED WALKS

Wanlockhead is on the Southern Upland Way and the Way's route can be followed from the village to the summit of Lowther Hill. The strange-looking 'golf ball' building on top of the hill houses radar equipment.

▶ *Continue on the **B797** and turn right at the **A76** to Sanquhar.*

4 **Sanquhar,** Dumfries and Galloway
Although there is a great deal of farmland around Sanquhar, it has the air of an industrial town and lies on the edge of the district's coal mining area. The ruins of Sanquhar Castle lie on the outskirts. The castle was built by the Ross family but sold to the Douglases of Drumlanrig in 1639. One of that family, the 1st Duke of Queensberry, built the mansion of Drumlanrig but spent only one night there and then retired to Sanquhar Castle. The finest building in the village is the Tolbooth, a splendid Georgian building topped by an octagonal cupola, a clock tower, and a weathercock. A double-sided staircase leads to a first-floor entrance. The busy main street boasts the oldest post office in Britain (1763) and a tall granite obelisk erected to commemorate the two Sanquhar Declarations. These were issued by the Covenanters in defiance of Charles II and James VII (II of Great Britain).

i   *Tolbooth, High Street (seasonal)*

▶ *Continue on the **A76** and turn right at the **B740**. Turn left at an unclassified road before Crawfordjohn; this road leads to Glespin, Douglas and Muirkirk. When this road meets the **A70**, turn right and follow this to Douglas, 19 miles (31km).*

5 **Douglas,** Strathclyde
The village is named after the Douglas family, the most famous member of whom was the 'Good' Sir James, so-called by the Scots because it was he who attempted to carry out Robert the Bruce's wish to have his heart taken to the Holy Land. Unfortunately he never got there, as he was killed in Spain. The English, however, knew him as 'Black Douglas' because he was such a ferocious fighter. His most barbaric act took place here in 1307 when he destroyed his own castle, then occupied by English troops. In a gruesome act that became known as the 'Douglas Larder', he made a great pile of

Crumbling stonework marks the site of the Castle of Sanquhar

all the food in the captured castle, poured on all the wine, killed all his prisoners and threw their bodies into the mix and set fire to it!

The 14th-century St Bride's Church, which has an attractive 16th-century octagonal clock tower, has a mausoleum in which lie the remains of the Good Sir James. The clock tower is the oldest working town clock in the country and was supposedly a gift from Mary, Queen of Scots in 1565. However, don't set your watch by its chimes as they sound three minutes before the hour, keeping faith with the Douglas motto 'Never behind'.

▶ *Return along the **A70** and continue on it to Muirkirk. Turn right at the **B743** and follow this to Strathaven.*

6 Strathaven, Strathclyde
Strathaven is the site of the 15th-century Avondale Castle. Beside it stands the Town Mill which ground flour until 1966,

but now serves as a theatre and arts centre. The town built its prosperity on the weaving industry and the John Hastie Museum contains displays on weaving and ceramics together with mementoes of the Covenanting times and the Radical Rising of 1820, one of whose leaders was a local man, James Wilson.

☐ *Town Mill Arts Centre, Stonehouse Road (seasonal)*

▶ *Take the **A723** for 7 miles (11km) to Hamilton.*

7 Hamilton, Strathclyde
Although Lanark was the county town of the former Lanarkshire, Hamilton became its administrative centre and its fine public buildings reflect its importance. The town's Muir Street museum, which is housed in a 17th-century coaching inn, has a very good transport section.

The parkland lying between the town and the

Formerly the Duke of Hamilton's hunting lodge, Chatelherault is today an impressive country park

motorway used to be the site of Hamilton Palace, which had to be demolished in 1927 as the extensive coal mine workings had weakened its foundations. However, the splendid 19th-century Adam-built Hamilton Mausoleum still stands here. When having a look around, it's worth noting the fine cupola and ornate carvings. Inside the building its 15-second echo is the longest of any building in Europe, a fact that put paid to its original purpose as a chapel. William Adam also designed the Duke of Hamilton's hunting lodge, Chatelherault, and this magnificent building, overlooks the district. The wooded gorge of the River Avon is impressive and beyond it are the remains of Cadzow Castle and some very ancient oaks.

☐ *Road Chef Services, M74 north-bound*

▶ *Leave by the A724 and follow this to Blantyre.*

8 Blantyre, Strathclyde
Blantyre was the home of the explorer David Livingstone and the David Livingstone Centre

relates his exploits, which included the 'discovery' of the Victoria Falls and Lake Nyasa. The centre is based in the row of 18th-century tenements where he was born.

▶ *Return along the A724, turn left at the A725 and join the B7071 to Bothwell. Bothwell Castle is signposted from the town.*

9 Bothwell Castle,
Strathclyde
The outstanding castle, which stands on a rocky promontory above the River Clyde, was partially completed before the outbreak of the Wars of Independence and was twice besieged and deliberately dismantled to deny it to the English. Later rebuilding in the late 14th and 15th centuries turned it into an impressive structure and the castle's donjon has walls 15 feet (5m) thick.

▶ *Return along the B7071, heading towards Hamilton. Follow the A724, then the A72 to Crossford. In the village, a signposted road on the right leads to Craignethan Castle, 13 miles (21km).*

Painting from the David Livingstone Centre, showing the explorer being attacked by a lion

10 Craignethan Castle,
Strathclyde
Craignethan Castle, a stronghold of the Hamiltons fervent supporters of Mary, Queen of Scots, was built in the 15th and 16th centuries when developments in artillery had made the defence systems of many castles obsolete. It was built with new defensive strategies in mind and it features a caponier, a low chamber set across the defensive ditch and reached by a stair from the castle wall, that allowed the defenders to rake the ditch with fire and so protect the vulnerable base of the castle walls.

▶ *Return to Crossford and turn right. Continue on the A72 for the 6-mile (10km) return to Lanark.*

Taking
the Waters

Water is an important feature of this tour which for some of the way follows the course of the Tweed, one of Scotland's greatest trout and salmon rivers. The tour starts in the village of Moffat which in the 17th-century gained importance as a spa after the discovery of suphurous springs there.

1/2 DAYS • 194KM • 120 MILES

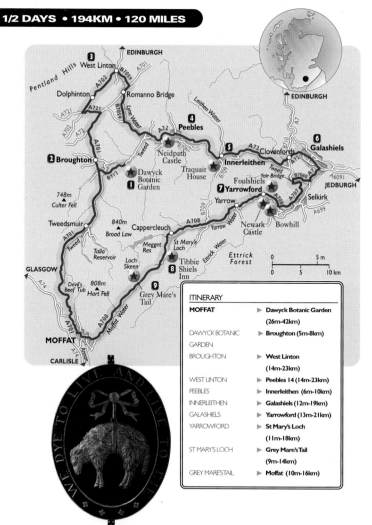

ITINERARY		
MOFFAT	►	**Dawyck Botanic Garden**
		(26m–42km)
DAWYCK BOTANIC GARDEN	►	**Broughton** (5m–8km)
BROUGHTON	►	**West Linton**
		(14m–23km)
WEST LINTON	►	**Peebles** 14 (14m–23km)
PEEBLES	►	**Innerleithen** (6m–10km)
INNERLEITHEN	►	**Galashiels** (12m–19km)
GALASHIELS	►	**Yarrowford** (13m–21km)
YARROWFORD	►	**St Mary's Loch**
		(11m–18km)
ST MARY'S LOCH	►	**Grey Mare's Tail**
		(9m–14km)
GREY MARE'S TAIL	►	**Moffat** (10m–16km)

i *Churchgate (seasonal)*

BACK TO NATURE

Scotland has a number of spa towns and Moffat has always been one of the most popular. The water is rather sulphurous – one writer compared it to a 'slightly putrescent egg'! Nevertheless, it has attracted many sufferers afflicted with lung infections, dyspepsia, rheumatism, and other disorders. The waters flow from the local greywacke rock, a type of limestone. The wells are signposted from the village, and are worth visiting.

▶ *Leave by the A701 and turn right at the B712 to Dawyck Garden.*

❶ Dawyck Botanic Garden, Borders

This outstation of the Royal Botanic Garden in Edinburgh was developed from the gardens laid out around Dawyck House during the last 300 years. Some of the conifers stand 130 feet

(40m) high. Daffodils are the main attraction in the spring, while autumn colour is provided by magnificent beeches and maples. Many unusual rhododendrons and narcisi can be found here. The gardens are closed in winter.

▶ *Return along the B712 and turn right at the A701. This leads to Broughton, 5 miles (8km).*

❷ Broughton, Borders

The John Buchan Centre is dedicated to the life and work of the novelist whose best-known works were *The 39 Steps* and *Greenmantle*. Apart from spy stories, he also wrote biographies of historical figures such as Sir Walter Scott and Oliver Cromwell. He later became Lord Tweedsmuir and was Governor-General of Canada until his death in 1940. The nearby Broughton Gallery is housed in a building resembling a 17th-century fortified tower, and contains a collection of the works of Edward Homel (1864-1933).

▶ *Continue on the A701 and turn right at the A72. Turn left at the A721 and right at the A702. Follow this to West Linton.*

❸ West Linton, Borders

West Linton was once busy with cattle drovers bringing their beasts over the Pentland Hills on their way to buyers in England, but today it is a peaceful little place, pleasant for strolling and exploring the narrow streets.

The village was famous for its stonemasons, who became the chief gravestone carvers in the area. Gifford's Stone, a bas relief on a wall in the main street, shows the stonemason James Gifford and his family. Opposite it is another of his works, the Lady Gifford Well, which was carved in 1666.

▶ *Leave by the B7059. Turn right at the A701 and left at the B7059. Turn left at the A72 for Peebles.*

Strolling in the tranquil and restful Dawyck Botanic Gardens

RECOMMENDED
WALKS

There is great scope for walking in this area and many parts of the Southern Upland Way provide well-marked paths that are straightforward to follow. For those who can organise transport at the end of the walks, The Way offers pleasant outings on the eastern shore of St Mary's Loch, from the loch to Traquair and from Traquair to Galashiels (via cairns known as the Three Brethren).

Peebles is the start of the Tweed Walk, where a choice of circular walks of different lengths allows walkers to pass Neidpath Castle and follow the river upstream, visiting various points of interest; contact the Tourist Information Centre for further details.

4 Peebles, Borders

This is certainly one of the Scottish Borders' most impressive towns, with an attractive position beside the River Tweed and a fine array of buildings along both sides of the main street. It developed under the protection of a royal castle and its modern prosperity came from tweed and knitwear. The Chambers Institute in High Street was given to Peebles by the publisher William Chambers who was born here. It dates from the 16th century and houses the war memorial which is in the rear garden. Further along the street stand fine buildings such as the Old Town House, the County Hotel and the Tontine Hotel. This last-named hotel was financed on the 'tontine' principle, whereby the last survivor of a group of investors fell heir to the property. At the top of High

The 14th century Neidpath Castle, overlooking the River Tweed

Street, the 15th-century mercat cross stands in the middle of the road.

One of the town's oldest buildings is the Old Cross Kirk, built in the 13th century on the order of King Aléxander III after the discovery of a 'magnificent and venerable' cross. From here, Cross Road leads to St Andrew's Tower, one of the few remains of a church that was built here in 1195. The surrounding graveyard has some beautifully carved headstones.

Neidpath Castle stands to the west of Peebles. This substantial five-storeyed building was built in the 14th century by the Hayes family and sits on a steep rocky crag overlooking the River Tweed.

[i] *High Street (seasonal)*

Ironmonger's shopfront in Peebles' main street.

▶ *Continue on the **A72** for 6 miles (10km) to Innerleithen.*

8 Innerleithen, Borders
The town's wells, which were associated with St Ronan, became very popular in the 19th century, helped enormously by Sir Walter Scott's novel *St Ronan's Well*. The poet James Hogg also played a role in publicising the village as he helped organise the St Ronan's Games from 1827 to 1835. The wells can still be visited and are found by following Hall Street and St Ronan's Terrace. This is the oldest spa in Scotland and the present pump-room was

built in 1826. The NTS has taken Robert Smail's Printing Works in the High Street under its care. This fascinating little print shop was started in 1840, when the original press was water-powered.

The settlement of Traquair is just over a mile (2km) south of Innerleithen. Its history goes back to Roman times when it was a town of similar importance to Peebles. Today it is best known for nearby Traquair House which is one of the country's oldest and most interesting inhabited houses. Additions were made in the 17th century by the first Earl of

The dining room at Traquair House, one of the country's oldest inhabited houses

Traquair after the course of the River Tweed was altered to safeguard the building's foundations. The most famous features of the house are the wrought iron 'Bear Gates' at the end of the driveway. These were closed in the 18th century by the fifth Earl, who promised they would not be reopened until another Stuart king was on the British throne.

▶ *Continue on the **A72** for 12 miles (19km) to Galashiels.*

6 Galashiels, Borders

Galashiels gained early importance when it was a hunting seat for the Scottish kings. However, its real growth came when woollen mills diverted Gala Water to power their machinery. This is now a busy town and one of the main centres of the Borders' textile industry. The story of the town mills is displayed in the Galashiels Museum and Exhibition which is housed in the Peter Anderson Mills; tours round these mills are available.

The town's most historic building is Old Gala House, which was founded around 1583; it has a fine painted ceiling of 1635. The mercat cross, which marks the centre of the old town, stands near to Gala House and was erected in 1695. As all the public business of the medieval town was conducted here, this is one of the places involved in the town's Braw Lads Gathering, the annual festival during which the boundaries of the town are ridden round on horseback.

The local war memorial is in the form of a statue of a

mounted Border 'reiver'. Although these men have become romanticised figures of legend, they were basically cattle thieves and their activities gave rise to the word 'blackmail' for payment as an 'insurance' that livestock would be safe from theft.

Spools of wool ready for working into cloth at the Peter Anderson Mills, Galashiels

> **SPECIAL TO . . .**
>
> Many of the towns have a justly famous reputation for producing high-quality knitted goods and many of the mills have their own shops where bargains can be found. Although it might be thought that the word 'tweed' (meaning the cloth) comes from the river of the same name that is not so. The word is said to have originated in 1832 from a one-time misreading in London of the word 'tweel' which was the name given locally to one of the types of cloth.

i 3 St John Street (seasonal)

▶ *Leave by the **A7** (to Selkirk). Turn right at the **B7060**, then left at the **A707** at Yair Bridge. Continue on this road which becomes the **A708** near Selkirk. Follow Ettrick Water and then Yarrow Water on the **A708** to Yarrowford.*

7 Yarrowford, Borders

The scattered village of Yarrowford lies by Yarrow Water, about which poet William Wordsworth wrote no less than three poems! Downstream of the village lie three buildings that are of interest: Newark Castle, Foulshiels and Bowhill.

The name Newark Castle signifies that it is the 'new work' which was erected to replace an unsuitable 'auld work'. It was constructed some time before 1423 as a royal hunting lodge in what was known as Ettrick Forest. The term 'forest' in this case does not necessarily imply the whole area had trees on it, but that special laws governed its use as a playground for the king and

his entourage. However, the forest was inhabited not only by deer and other wild animals; it made a splendid hiding place for thieves, until such time as the king decided to chase them as well! In the 16th century, James V replaced 10,000 deer with an equal number of sheep, greatly increasing the importance of sheep farming and the woollen industry in the area. In conjunction with this step, many trees were felled – thus destroying the oak, birch and hazel forest that had prospered here since the end of the Ice Age.

Foulshiels was the birthplace of the Scots explorer Mungo Park who travelled through West Africa between 1795 and 1796 in search of the source of the River Niger. His exploits were described in his book *Travels in the Interior of Africa*, but his second trip into these uncharted lands led to his death.

Bowhill House and Country Park features a very large country mansion built in the early 19th century. It has an outstanding collection of French furniture as well as a large collection of paintings by Old Masters including Van Dyck, Canaletto and Gainsborough.

The aptly-named Grey Mare's Tail waterfall

▶ *Continue on the A708 to the southern end of St Mary's Loch.*

8 St Mary's Loch, Borders

This is one of the largest lochs in southern Scotland and it is a popular place with walkers, boating enthusiasts and anglers. At the southern end of the loch stands a monument to the local poet James Hogg. He was a good friend of Sir Walter Scott and the two of them, along with other literary figures, spent convivial evenings in the nearby Tibbie Shiels Inn.

▶ *Continue on the A708 for 9 miles (14km) to the car-park at the Grey Mare's Tail waterfall.*

9 Grey Mare's Tail, Dumfries and Galloway

Just a short distance from the roadside, the Tail Burn tumbles 200 feet (60m) over the waterfall known as the Grey Mare's Tail. A path runs up the eastern bank of the burn offering different views of the waterfall and the opportunity to explore Loch Skene. Leaflets warn about the dangers of leaving the path. The burn joins attractive Moffat Water, whose valley the road follows towards Moffat. The valley is a magnificent textbook example of a glacial valley, with its U-shape formed as the glacier smoothed the mountainsides.

▶ *Continue on the A708 for 10 miles (16km) in order to return to Moffat.*

FOR HISTORY BUFFS

Sir Walter Scott, writer of so many 'romantic' stories of Scotland, is connected with many places in this district. He often visited the village of Clovenfords and a statue of him stands there; he lived at the house of Ashiestiel (further down the Tweed from Innerleithen) from 1804 to 1812; and he had his last meeting with James Hogg at the Gordon Arms (east of St Mary's Loch) in 1830.

SCENIC ROUTES

Much of this tour goes through beautiful countryside as it winds its way through the hills of the Southern Uplands. Perhaps the nicest stretches are north of Moffat (look out for the large depression called the Devil's Beef Tub, where Border cattle-rustlers once hid their ill-gotten gains, between the Tweedsmuir and the Lowther hills), and through the valleys of the Yarrow Water and the Moffat Water.

Walter Scott
Country

Much of the countryside explored in this tour was the inspiration behind Sir Walter Scott's *Waverley* novels: the ruined abbeys of Melrose, Dryburgh and Jedburgh; the Eildon Hills. It is only fitting, therefore, that this tour should end with a visit to Scott's home.

1/2 DAYS • 187KM • 116 MILES

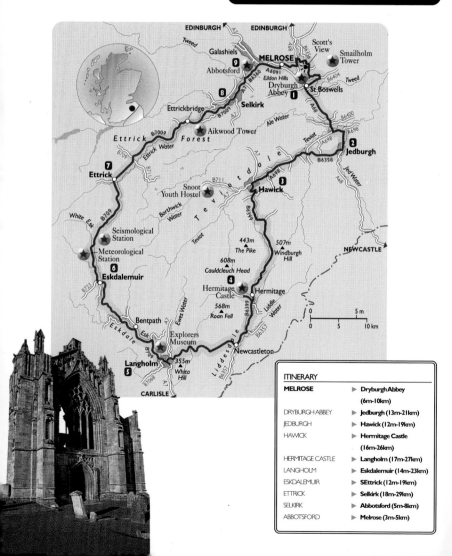

ITINERARY		
MELROSE	▶	**Dryburgh Abbey**
		(6m-10km)
DRYBURGH ABBEY	▶	**Jedburgh (13m-21km)**
JEDBURGH	▶	**Hawick (12m-19km)**
HAWICK	▶	**Hermitage Castle**
		(16m-26km)
HERMITAGE CASTLE	▶	**Langholm (17m-27km)**
LANGHOLM	▶	**Eskdalemuir (14m-23km)**
ESKDALEMUIR	▶	**SEttrick (12m-19km)**
ETTRICK	▶	**Selkirk (18m-29km)**
SELKIRK	▶	**Abbotsford (5m-8km)**
ABBOTSFORD	▶	**Melrose (3m-5km)**

The heart of Robert the Bruce is buried within the imposing ruins of Melrose Abbey

i *Abbey House (seasonal)*

▶ *Leave Melrose by the B6361 and turn left at the A68. Cross the River Tweed, then turn first right and first left. Head towards Dryburgh following the B6356. Turn right after passing Scott's View and continue to Dryburgh Abbey.*

❶ **Dryburgh Abbey,**
Borders

Much of the abbey's substantial ruins date from the 12th and 13th centuries and they occupy a wonderfully peaceful position on a horseshoe bend of the River Tweed. Founded in 1150, the abbey suffered at the hands of the English raiders but nevertheless remains the most complete of the Border abbeys. The grave of Sir Walter Scott can be found in the north transept. A short woodland walk leads to a massive 19th-century statue of the Scottish patriot Sir William Wallace.

To the northwest of the abbey (and reached via the B6404) stands the very attractive Smailholm Tower. This was erected in the 16th century as a defensive structure, which explains why the few windows it has are very small. There is a marvellous panoramic view from it and ships approaching Berwick once used it as a landmark as it was so conspicuous. During medieval times this area was often attacked by English forces and tall towers were needed to spy on the movements of the enemy and to warn others of the approach of an attacking force. This is why the parapet wall has a watchman's seat and a recess for a lantern, in accordance with an Act of Council in 1587 which stated that castle owners must 'keep watch nyght and day, and burn baillis (bales) according to the accoustomat ordour observit as sic tymes upoun the borderis'. At one time it was owned by Sir Walter Scott's grandfather and Scott used to visit here as a boy; he later featured the tower in *Marmion*.

▶ *Return to the **B6356** and continue following that road. Turn right at the **B6404** and enter St Boswells. Turn left at the **A68** and follow it to Jedburgh.*

2 **Jedburgh,** Borders
The town's location close to the border meant that it was forever being attacked by the English, and its castle was often under siege by the ancient enemy. The locals, fed up with all this harassment, managed to persuade the Scottish parliament to pull the castle down in 1409, thus relieving them of the task of having to fight the invaders to defend it! The

Jedburgh Abbey was founded in the 12th century and colonised by monks from Beauvais in France

present building occupying the site is still called the 'castle' but it was built in the 19th century as a gaol and is now used as a museum.

The other major building in the town is Jedburgh Abbey, founded as a priory in 1138. After various attacks by the English, the building was destroyed by them between 1545 and 1546. However, the abbey walls still soar skywards and the tower stands as it did when rebuilt in 1504 to 1508. Mary, Queen of Scots visited the town in 1566 and stayed in the Spread Eagle Hotel in High Street which is claimed to be the oldest continually occupied hotel in the country. A fire here forced Mary to leave and she stayed at what is now the Mary, Queen of Scots' House, a fine 16th-century fortified house.

i *Murray's Green*

Priorwood Gardens, where a large variety of plants are grown especially for drying

BACK TO NATURE

Just north of Jedburgh, Harestanes Countryside Visitor Centre offers walks, a wildlife garden and demonstrations of traditional crafts. Melrose's Priorwood Garden, which is run by the NTS, specialises in dried flowers. A bewildering variety of plants, both large and small, are grown and dried here and there is always lots of valuable advice to be had on this craft. A small herb garden has also been established and there is an orchard with a wide variety of apple trees, arranged to illustrate the history of the fruit. The monks of Melrose Abbey established their orchards at Gattonside, just over the Tweed from the Abbey.

▶ *Leave by the **B6358**, then join the **A698** to Hawick.*

3 Hawick, Borders

Hawick is the largest and busiest of the Border towns. Its numerous woollen mills have brought it much prosperity since frame knitting was introduced here and commercialised in 1771. When mechanisation came to the industry, production changed from hose to fine underwear, which as the advertisements of the day put it, 'enjoyed the patronage of many of the crowned heads of Europe!'

Many of the mills stand by the River Teviot, their original source of power. The river also flows past Wilton Lodge Park, in which stands the museum and art gallery which has displays on Border history, the knitwear industry and natural history.

ⓘ Drumlanrig's Tower

▶ *Leave by the **B6399**. Just after Hermitage, turn right at the unclassified road signposted to Hermitage Castle.*

4 Hermitage Castle, Borders

This must be one of the grimmest-looking castles in Scotland, with its very small windows and the high arch that joins the east and west towers together. It it also sited on an isolated expanse of moorland, well away from any settlement.

In 1566, when she was holding court at Jedburgh, Mary, Queen of Scots heard that her lover Bothwell was lying wounded in the castle. She rode the 20 miles (32km) here at a furious speed, stayed for a couple of hours then returned, an exertion that cost her a 10-day fever.

▶ *Return to the **B6399** and turn right. Turn right at the **B6357** and enter Newcastleton. Within the village, turn right at the minor road to Langholm and turn left when you join the **A7**, 17 miles (27km).*

5 Langholm, Dumfries and Galloway

This small town sits at the confluence of the Esk, Ewes and Wauchope Waters. There is a fine view of it from the summit of Whita Hill (to the east), on

6 Eskdalemuir, Dumfries and Galloway

There is a settlement at Eskdalemuir (at the junction of the Langholm and Lockerbie roads), but the name is more commonly used for the great moorland near the upper reaches of the White Esk. To be correct, it used to be a great moorland, but the land is now given over to huge conifer plantations.

The Romans built an important road here, some 24 feet (7m) wide, and this eventually led to Trimontium, near Melrose. The most intriguing group of modern incomers were Tibetan abbots who left their country in 1959 and settled here in Johnstone House. The community they founded flourished and they later built one of Scotland's most remarkable buildings, the Samye Ling Temple, a colourful four-storey structure. This is the largest Buddhist temple in western Europe and numerous examples of Tibetan art can be seen inside.

The meteorological station at Eskdalemuir is sited further along the road. This was origi-

top of which there is a monument to Sir John Malcolm. Close to the start of the path to the monument, there is a rather interesting (or bizarre, depending on your taste) monument dedicated to the modern Scots poet Christopher Murray Grieve, who wrote under the pen-name Hugh McDiarmid.

Another of Langholm's sons was the great engineer Thomas Telford, whose famous designs include the Caledonian Canal, the Menai Straits Bridge and St Katharine's Docks in London. Many roads and bridges in Scotland are also his. Telford started his working life as a stonemason, and an archway, an early example of his own handiwork, can be seen beside the town hall. A memorial to him is sited at Bentpath, on the road to

Eskdalemuir.

Just north of Langholm, the Craigcleuch Scottish Explorers Museum has a large collection of artefacts from many countries visited by Scottish explorers.

The Old Manse at Ettrick

nally founded in 1908 to continue the terrestrial magnetism measurements formerly made at Kew (in London). A seismological station has been established near by.

▶ *Continue on the B709 to Ettrick.*

7 Ettrick, Borders
The collection of houses and farms at Ettrick is found where the B709 meets Ettrick Water at Ramseycleuch. The poet James Hogg was born here and a tall sandstone memorial at his birthplace can be found on the roadside by following Ettrick Water upstream. Hogg is one of the Borders' most famous characters and was affectionately known as the Ettrick Shepherd. His poetry was first published in 1794 and he went on to write countless poems, articles and books. Ettrick's church is further upstream and this is where Hogg is buried. Beside his headstone is one inscribed 'Here lyeth William Laidlaw the far-famed Will o'Phaup who for feats of frolic, agility and strength had no equal in his day'. This gentleman was

Hogg's grandfather and he was the last man in Ettrick to speak to the fairies. There is a James Hogg Exhibition at Aikwood Tower, further along on the B7009.

▶ *Continue on the B709. Turn right at the B7009 to enter Selkirk.*

8 Selkirk, Borders
The town occupies a hilly site where a Tironensian abbey was founded around 1113. The abbey was eventually moved to Roxburgh and then to Kelso, so Selkirk never developed as a religious centre like the other Border towns which had their splendid abbeys. As the town grew it became famous for its shoemaking, to the extent that its burgesses were given the name 'souters' (Scots for 'shoemakers'). This trade died out and Selkirk's modern prosperity is based on the woollen mills beside Ettrick Water. The centre of the town is at the triangular-shaped marketplace dominated by a statue of Sir Walter Scott. Behind is the museum in the Town Hall which features the old court-

Sir Walter Scott's romantic creation, Abbotsford House

room containing Scott's bench and chair from the time when he was Sheriff of Selkirkshire.
    The local museum in Halliwell's House is to the west of the marketplace and is reached through a narrow lane. The museum has an excellent display of local material including the reconstructed interior of an old ironmonger's shop.
    To the east of the marketplace, and past the statue of the explorer Mungo Park, is the Flodden Memorial, dedicated to the local men who perished at the Battle of Flodden in 1513. The statue is of a man called Fletcher, reputedly the only Selkirk man out of 80 to return from the battle, carrying a captured English standard.

⌐i⌐ *Halliwell's House (seasonal)*

▶ *Leave by the A7 and head towards Galashiels. Turn right at the B6360 to reach Abbotsford.*

9 Abbotsford, Borders
Sir Walter Scott bought the site

on which he built Abbotsford in 1811. The house took a long time to complete as he kept adding bits on, eventually ending up with a great variety of styles. Basically, it is of Scots baronial style but he included a 16th-century door from Edinburgh's Tolbooth, a copy of a porch at Linlithgow Palace and even medieval gargoyles. He was a romantic in his architectural taste as well as his writings. The house also contains wonderful memorabilia, such as a gun belonging to Rob Roy, and a cup which Bonnie Prince Charlie carried around with him.

Scott was a lawyer and served as Sheriff in Selkirk. He assiduously collected and wrote down the oral tradition of the old Border tales that had been handed down through the generations, thus ensuring that many of them were preserved. He also began to write his own material and started to make a reputation for himself as a poet and then as a novelist. His best-known works include *Kenilworth*, *Redgauntlet* and

Abbotsford house: interior

Ivanhoe. Unfortunately, the financial collapse of a publisher landed him with huge personal debts of about £114,000 which he tried to work off; sadly his exertions led to his untimely death in 1832.

▶ Continue on the **B6360** and turn right at the **A6091** for 3 miles (5km) for Melrose.

The walled garden at Abbotsford House

The Border
Country

Few cities match Edinburgh's city centre: Princes Street and its gardens; Edinburgh Castle; the Royal Mile, with its medieval 'lands', or blocks of flats; the Palace of Holyroodhouse, and the elegant Georgian architecture of New Town. The best view of all the city's treasures is from Arthur's Seat, a volcanic hill 823 feet (251m) above sea level.

2 DAYS • 239KM • 148 MILES

Princes Street at sunset

---

i *3 Princes Street*

▶ *Leave by the A1 and turn left at the A198 to reach Gullane.*

❶ Gullane, Lothian
Gullane is renowned as a golfing centre, with a number of courses including a championship course at nearby Muirfield.

Further east, the centre of the old village of Dirleton, claimed to be the most beautiful village in Scotland, is dominated by the grand Dirleton Castle which dates back to the 13th century. Perched on top of a rocky platform, it has massive towers and was defended by a moat at least 50 feet (15m) wide.

▶ *Continue on the A198 for 5 miles (8km) to North Berwick.*

❷ North Berwick, Lothian
This seaside golf resort is dominated by the nearby 613-foot (187m) North Berwick Law, which offers fine views over the town and the coast.

The town's main antiquity is the ruin of the old church of St Andrews, where in 1591 the story goes that a gathering of witches and wizards was addressed by the Devil in the form of a black goat. They sought the death of James VI and a number of these 'plotters' were subsequently brought to trial and burned at the stake. The Devil (who may have been the heavily disguised Earl of Bothwell) escaped a similar fate.

i *Quality Street*

▶ *Continue on the A198 and turn left at a signposted minor road to Tantallon Castle, 3 miles (5km).*

❸ Tantallon Castle, Lothian
This grim-looking 14th century castle stands in a spectacular clifftop position, with three sides protected by the sea and the fourth by thick walls. Two great sieges took place here: the first ended by negotiation (the attackers had run out of gunpowder!) and in the second, General Monk attacked it for 12 days in 1651, damaging the towers. This is the best place on the mainland to view the Bass Rock. The island has huge numbers of gannets there and the colony is so important that the birds' scientific name *Sula bassana* comes from the island.

Whale jaw crowning the top of Berwick Law

▶ *Return to the A198 and continue southwards. Turn right at the B1407 to enter Preston.*

4 Preston, Lothian
On the outskirts of the village stands the charming 18th-century water-driven Preston Mill. Originally a meal mill, the unusual design of its kiln has similarities with an English oast house. The buildings are constructed of orange sandstone rubble and roofed with traditional east coast pantiles. A short walk leads to the Phantassie Doocot, a dovecot which once housed some 500 pigeons.

▶ *Leave by the B1047 and turn left on to the B1377. Turn left at the A1, then left at the A1087 to Dunbar.*

5 Dunbar, Lothian
This popular seaside resort is now a rather peaceful place, a far cry from the turbulent times when its castle was of some importance. The castle was eventually sacked by Cromwell

in 1650 and its walls torn down, the stones being used to improve the harbour. The remains sit quite forlornly by the harbour entrance. The attractive harbour is home to a busy fishing fleet and there is a nearby lifeboat museum. John Muir, the conservationist, was born in Dunbar in the mid-19th century.

i 143 High Street

▶ *Continue on the A1087 and turn left at the A1 to Cockburnspath.*

6 Cockburnspath, Borders
The position of this village, which is so close to the border, has meant a turbulent and rather troubled history. This was an important stopping point for horse-drawn coaches (a mode of travel which peaked in the 19th century) and the layout of the village and its marketplace owes much to this time. The parish church is worth a look; it has a fine tower in the middle of the west gable and an unusual sundial on the southwest corner.

The mercat cross is the finishing point of the Southern Upland Way, the long distance footpath that starts at

Portpatrick, over on the west coast. By following the Southern Upland Way from its terminus, you will find yourself by a group of houses at Cove, below which is the picturesque Cove Harbour. The harbour is reached by going through a tunnel cut into the cliff; this was made in the 18th century and was connected to cellars probably used for curing and barrelling fish, and possibly by smugglers.

Preston's Phantassie Doocot, once home to over 500 pigeons and now home to considerably less

The cliffs at St Abbs Head are home to countless kittiwakes, guillemots, razorbills and other seabirds. A marked path starts from just before St Abbs village and leads past the bird cliffs, allowing a very good view of the colonies – but stick to the path!

▶ Continue on the **A1** and turn left at the **A1107**. At Coldingham, turn left at the **B6438** and follow this to St Abbs.

7 St Abbs, Borders

This neat little fishing village is now a resort, often busy with divers who come to explore the local bays.

Nearby Coldingham has an ancient priory. Founded in 1098 by King Edgar, the 13th-century priory church was built on a site that had a religious house way back in the 7th century. Life could hardly have been peaceful for those that stayed here during the frequent outbreaks of hostilities, as the monks were subject to the English king and the priors to the Scots king!

▶ Return along the **B6438** to Coldingham and turn left at the **A1107**. Turn left at the **B6355** for Eyemouth.

8 Eyemouth, Borders

This busy fishing port has regular fish markets which are worth visiting. This is home to a large fleet and the local people have been connected with fishing for a very long time. The town's saddest day came on 14 October 1881 when a sudden gale blew up and 129 local fishermen were drowned, some of them in full sight of anxious families watching from the shore. The local museum tells the story of the fishing tragedy.

_i_ Auld Kirk (seasonal)

▶ Return along the **B6355**, then follow the **A6105** to Duns.

Tapestry from Eyemouth museum, showing the 1881 fishing tragedy

The picturesque little harbour at St Abbs

9 Duns, Borders

This long-established village, with its well-built stone houses, makes a useful stopping point for touring this part of the Borders. Duns was the home town of the world motor-racing champion Jim Clark, who died in a race in Germany in 1968; a small museum has mementoes of his short but fascinating life. A short drive away from Duns is the mansion Manderston, with formally laid-out gardens and a marble dairy, both of which are worth a tour.

▶ Leave on the **A6112** for 12 miles (19km) to reach Coldstream.

10 Coldstream, Borders

Coldstream stands on the banks of the River Tweed, which at this point marks the border with England. The river is crossed by a magnificent seven-arch bridge and on the Scottish side a toll house was the east coast equivalent of Gretna Green, a place where marriages could take place with the minimum of delay. Like so many other little towns in the Borders, Coldstream has a wealth of well-built houses. The Market Square is a little off this street and in it can be found the Coldstream Museum, which tells the story of the town and the Coldstream Guards regiment.

Outside Coldstream stands the Hirsel Homestead Museum comprising a museum, craft centre and walks in the estate.

i High Street (seasonal)

▶ *Leave by the A697 and turn left at the A698 to reach Kelso.*

11 Kelso, Borders

Kelso has one of the most attractive town centres in the Borders, with a huge open square that has often been likened to that of a French town. The town stands at the confluence of the rivers Teviot and Tweed and from the fine bridge which crosses the Tweed there is a good view of Floors Castle, a huge mansion built by William Adam between 1721 and 1725, offering glittering excesses of fine French furniture, porcelain and paintings. Kelso Abbey was once the Borders' greatest abbey but only the west end of it stands today. It was founded here in 1128 but its position on the 'invasion route' meant that it suffered frequent attacks. North of Kelso, Mellerstain House is one of Scotland's finest Robert Adam mansions.

i The Square (seasonal)

▶ *Leave by the A6089. Turn left at the A697 and left at the B6362. Follow this to Lauder.*

12 Lauder, Borders

This attractive town has a wide main street in the middle of which stands the Tolbooth. This was originally built in 1318 and the ground floor was used as a gaol up to 1840. Lauder's parish church is an interesting structure in the form of a Greek cross with an octagonal steeple and four arms; it is dated 1673. Impressive Thirlestane Castle stands close to the town and houses the Border Country Life Exhibitions.

The village of Earlston lies only a few miles south of Lauder. This was Ercildoune in medieval days and the home of Thomas the Rhymer who lived during the 13th century. His ability to see into the future was reckoned to be a gift from the Queen of the Fairies with whom it was believed he stayed for a number of years.

▶ *Take the A68 north to Pathhead, then turn left at the B6367 to Crichton Castle.*

13 Crichton Castle, Lothian

Crichton was at one time the home of the Earl of Bothwell, the ill-fated third husband of Mary, Queen of Scots. The ruins of this substantial structure stand

The surviving ruin of Kelso Abbey, showing fine Norman detail

on the edge of Middleton Moor and above the Tyne Water. It dates from the 14th century and one architectural curiosity is a Renaissance-influenced wall erected in the late 16th century. This is an arcade of seven bays topped by diamond-patterned stone-work and is unique in the country. Crichton's church is a fine building which was restored in 1896.

▶ *Return along the B6367 to Pathhead. Turn left and follow the A68 to Edinburgh.*

FOR CHILDREN

There are a number of good beaches, notably at Gullane Bay. Indoor swimming pools are located in Kelso, Duns, Dunbar and Eyemouth and there is an outdoor one at North Berwick. Pony trekking is available at Earlston, Ford (near Pathhead) and Westruther (east of Lauder). Crumstane Farm, near Duns, has many animals to interest children, from goats and geese to Clydesdale horses.

CENTRAL SCOTLAND

Black Mount and the Rannoch
Moors, seen from the River Bá

The great firths of the Clyde, the Forth and the Tay have narrowed the middle of Scotland to a thin neck of land only 30 miles (48km) wide. This is where the majority of the Scots live, in an area rich with history. Bronze Age cemeteries, medieval castles, historic battlefields and architectural follies all have their statements to make about their builders' views of the world and how they lived – and died.

Much of the region's history has been bloody. Land- and sea-borne invaders attacked, plundered and wrought destruction. But many invaders stayed and left their mark, often introducing foreign influences that have added to the common heritage of the modern Scottish nation. The Celts, Vikings, French and the peoples of the countries washed by the Baltic and the North Sea have all contributed to the country's history, but it has been the English who, despite being the 'auld enemy', have in so many ways changed the country – and also radically influenced how the Scots see themselves today as a nation.

Central Scotland's modern prosperity was based on the Industrial Revolution and many would argue that this was where that important period of history began. One of the world's first major ironworks, the first major use of efficient steam engines, the world's biggest shipbuilding industry – all of these were based right here.

Although the manufacturing industry has declined, the outstanding engineering marvels of Scotland are now today's tourist attractions in their own right. Eighteenth-century ironworks, 19th-century canals and the world's most famous railway bridge – spanning the Firth of Forth – are all showpieces of an industrial nation's genius for design. The region can also boast many architectural gems: the rich legacy of Victorian buildings in Glasgow, the grand country houses designed in Scots baronial style and the distinctive cottages of farmer and fisherman all display a very Scottish flavour. Glasgow itself has enjoyed regeneration in recent years, and now takes its rightful place as one of Europe's most lively and interesting cities. But it is the quality of life that matters more than bricks and mortar and one of the greatest attractions of the populated areas is their closeness to the hills and glens of the Highlands. The hills are never far away and even Glasgow, the country's industrial 'capital', has the Campsie Fells only a few miles from its centre.

Tour 8

Although this route is only a couple of hours' drive away from the industrial heartland of Scotland, it nevertheless encompasses some superb Highland scenery. The highly indented coastline, backed by 3000-foot (900m) high hills, provides a backdrop to some fascinating places like the 5000-year-old cairns at Kilmartin, medieval castles and the picturesque setting of Crinan Canal.

Tour 9

The Cowal peninsula is made up of a group of narrow peninsulas shaped like a grasping hand trying to grip the northern shore of the island of Bute. The narrow, twisting roads of Cowal give ever-changing vistas over the sea lochs and the great estuary of the Firth of Clyde, the busy waterway that linked the local communities before the arrival of the railway and the motor car.

Tour 10

The 'border' between the Highlands and the Lowlands is studded with lochs gouged out of the landscape by long-lost glaciers. Some of the country's best-known lochs are found here, and today's visitors follow in the footsteps of the 19th-century tourists, eager to sample the 'wild' scenery so vividly romanticised by Sir Walter Scott.

Tour 11

This historic corner of Scotland has an abundance of important buildings that armies fought over for centuries. Abbeys, grand palaces and austere castles were the prizes sought by the warring parties, and Stirling, the 'gateway to the Highlands', was the jewel in the crown that invaders tried to capture and that the Scots defended to the last. The battle sites excavated here testify to the lives sacrificed in the centuries of turmoil. But some places can often evade change and the small coastal town of Culross retains a rich legacy in its preserved buildings that time just passed by.

Tour 12

A rich agricultural area, Strathmore provides the background to this tour which skirts the southern limits of the Grampian Highlands. Prosperous farming communities, busy east coast fishing ports and the industrial town of Dundee all add their interest. In many ways this area is one of Scotland's 'hidden gems', as it is often missed by visitors who are more intent on heading straight for the Highlands.

Tour 13

Although never a separate legal entity, Fife earned the title 'Kingdom of Fife' through the influence of its ancient abbey in Dunfermline and later its medieval university in St Andrews. Cut off from the rest of the country by the great firths of the Forth and the Tay, it has a character that is very different from the rest of Scotland. This is most evident in its traditional architecture, especially the small white stone buildings with their pantiled roofs that are such a common feature in the many picturesque fishing villages of the East Neuk.

The cantilevered Forth Rail Bridge at dusk

TOUR
8

Argyll
Coast & Castles

Oban is still a thriving fishing port and the gateway to the Inner Hebrides. From Oban the tour winds along the dramatic coastline and then goes inland to the heart of the Highlands and Glen Coe, site of Scotland's most infamous massacre.

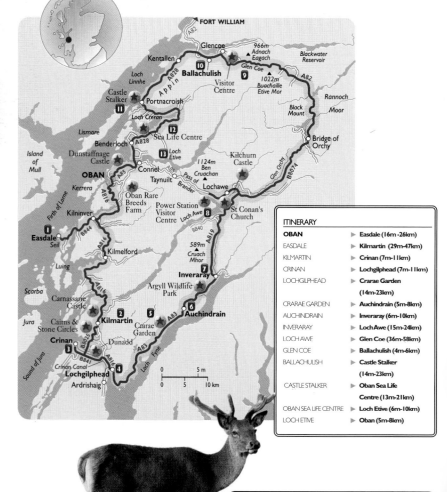

ITINERARY

OBAN	▶	Easdale (16m -26km)
EASDALE	▶	Kilmartin (29m-47km)
KILMARTIN	▶	Crinan (7m-11km)
CRINAN	▶	Lochgilphead (7m-11km)
LOCHGILPHEAD	▶	Crarae Garden (14m-23km)
CRARAE GARDEN	▶	Auchindrain (5m-8km)
AUCHINDRAIN	▶	Inveraray (6m-10km)
INVERARAY	▶	Loch Awe (15m-24km)
LOCH AWE	▶	Glen Coe (36m-58km)
GLEN COE	▶	Ballachulish (4m-6km)
BALLACHULISH	▶	Castle Stalker (14m-23km)
CASTLE STALKER	▶	Oban Sea Life Centre (13m-21km)
OBAN SEA LIFE CENTRE	▶	Loch Etive (6m-10km)
LOCH ETIVE	▶	Oban (5m-8km)

2/3 DAYS • 286KM • 177 MILES

54

FOR CHILDREN

An animal-based attraction is the Oban Rare Breeds Farm Park with its collection of pigs, sheep and cattle.

The Argyll Wildlife Park near Inveraray boasts many animals including wildcats, badgers, wild boar and deer.

BACK TO NATURE

Oban Bay can be seen from the town's harbour. Look for common seals , black guillemots and eiders. There is a nature trail at nearby Glen Nant 10 miles northeast via the B845, south of Taynuilt. Look for wood warblers, redstarts and roe deer in the woodlands

i Boswell House, Argyll Square

▶ *Head south on the A816, then turn right at the B844 which leads to Easdale (16 miles/26km).*

⓪ Easdale, Strathclyde

The village of Easdale lies on the island of Seil, connected to the mainland by the humped bridge known as the 'Bridge over the Atlantic'. The village shares its name with a little

Quarriers' houses lining the harbour at Easdale

island just offshore which houses a museum.

Easdale was a slate quarrying centre and the rows of quarriers' houses look much as they did in the 19th century. The quarries reached below sea level and in 1881 a ferocious sea broke their walls and flooded the workings; no repairs could be made and the industry never recovered.

▶ *Return along the B844 and turn right at the A816 and follow this to Kilmartin.*

❷ Kilmartin, Strathclyde

The area around the small village of Kilmartin has some of Scotland's most outstanding large cairns, forming a huge 'linear cemetery' that follows the Kilmartin Burn. West of the village is the massive Bronze Age Glebe Cairn and southwest of the village are the three Nether Largie Cairns. The cairns were used as tombs from around 5,000 years ago with bodies or cremated remains interred in stone-clad cells ('cists') within the cairns. A little further to the southwest lie the two Temple Wood Stone Circles.

Kilmartin Church's graveyard contains many celebrated sculptured gravestones, including the Poltalloch Stones, the gravestones of the Malcolm chiefs. Other large carved stones (the 'Kilmartin Crosses')

Stone circle at Temple Wood, near Kilmartin

can be seen inside the church.

The 16th-century fortified house known as Carnassarie Castle, can be seen on a hill just before the village. 8a)

▶ *Continue on the A816, then turn on to the B8025 to meet the Crinan Canal. Turn right at the B841 and follow it to Crinan.*

3 Crinan, Strathclyde

The Crinan Canal was opened in 1801 so boats could avoid the cruel seas around the Mull of Kintyre. This was a great boon to fishermen as the shortcut was only 8½ miles (14km) long compared to the sea route of 130 miles (200km). The advent of steamships dealt the canal a severe blow, but the canal is still in use today and can be busy with pleasure craft.

▶ *Return along the B841, which follows the canal. Join the A816 and follow it to Lochgilphead, 7 miles (11km).*

4 Lochgilphead, Strathclyde

The town developed as an administrative centre for the region and also because of the trade brought by the canal. A popular attraction today is a tour of the local Highbank Pottery.

ⓘ *Lochnell Street (seasonal)*

▶ *Leave by the A83 for 14 miles (23km) to Crarae Garden.*

Inveraray Castle, obviously modelled on the romantic French châteaux

5 Crarae Garden, Strathclyde

The garden was founded in 1912 in a steep-sided gorge and today has a rich collection of rhododendrons, magnolias, azaleas and many other trees and shrubs from around the world. The warmth of the Gulf Stream and an annual rainfall of 75 inches (190cm) help ensure that the garden delights visitors throughout the year, especially in early summer (for the rhododendrons) and in autumn.

▶ *Continue on the A83 for 5 miles (8km) to Auchindrain, just beyond the village of Furnace.*

6 Auchindrain, Strathclyde

Queen Victoria visited this little Highland township in 1875 and was impressed enough to record it in her diary. Today, the houses, barns, smiddy (traditional term for blacksmith) and other buildings of this fascinating community have been preserved as an open air folklife museum to show how people have lived here through the centuries.

▶ *Continue on the A83 for 6 miles (10km) to Inveraray.*

7 Inveraray, Strathclyde

This neat and well-planned village on Loch Fyne has been a royal burgh since 1648, but its 'modern' planning dates back to the middle of the 18th century, and the houses have been little changed in outward appearance since then.

The large parish church dominates the centre of the village and is sited in the middle of the main road. It was built at the turn of the 18th century with a central dividing wall so that services in Gaelic and English could be conducted simultaneously.

The fascinating Inveraray Jail Museum consists of the former courthouse (with actors in period costume) and two prisons. The older of the two was

'Let's be havin' yer' – jail museum at Inveraray

erected in 1820 as the Argyll County Prison and the newer one was built to 'modern' standards in 1849. The cells feature displays explaining the harshness of prison life and the appalling conditions the prisoners were kept in. Near the gaol are the 'lands', rows of houses reminiscent of some old Edinburgh houses. Neil Munro, author of the Para Handy tales, was born close by.

Inveraray Castle stands a short distance away from the village. The present building is mid-18th-century and replaces a castle built by Colin Campbell in about 1415. This is the home of the Dukes of Argyll, chiefs of Clan Campbell, and it has many exhibits relating to the clan's history.

i *Front Street*

SPECIAL TO ...

Fresh seafood is a speciality of the region. Crabs, prawns and lobsters should be available in many restaurants and Loch Fyne is famous for its herrings. Herrings were once given the alternative name of 'Glasgow Magistrates' as the quality of those sold in the city had to be approved by the magistrates. Indeed, the city used to give barrels of these delicious fish to people who rendered the city a great service!

▶ *Leave by the A819 and turn left at the A85 for Loch Awe.*

8 Loch Awe, Strathclyde
Loch Awe is dominated by the massive Ben Cruachan, a mountain with a pump storage hydroelectric power station inside it. Visits into the heart of the mountain start from the visitor centre (west along the A85). At the head of the loch stands the imposing ruin of Kilchurn Castle, a Campbell stronghold

The Three Sisters in Glen Coe, Scotland's most infamous glen

Winter sun on the hills around Kilchurn Castle on the banks of Loch Awe

RECOMMENDED WALKS

There are many walks in Argyll suitable for family outings, for example on the western shore of Loch Awe. The Crinan Canal towpath also provides pleasant walks, with lots to see when boats are passing through the locks.

built in the 15th and 17th centuries. It was abandoned in the 18th century and in 1879 a hurricane blew down the top of the tower that can be seen lying in the courtyard.

The intriguing St Conan's Church sits below the southeastern slopes of Ben Cruachan. This was started in 1881 and

added to over the next 50 years. It has elaborate carvings, including fragments from Iona Abbey, rich woodwork and a rare mixture of styles.

▶ *Return eastwards along the A85, then bear left at the B8074 towards Bridge of Orchy. Turn left at the A82 and follow it across Rannoch Moor to Glen Coe.*

9 Glen Coe, Highland
Glen Coe itself is regarded by many Scots as the country's finest glen and, no matter whether the sun is shining or the sky is black, it provides dramatic scenery that is difficult to better.

SCENIC ROUTES

There can be few journeys in Scotland more exciting than that through Glen Coe. The route to it is over Rannoch Moor, a high peaty wasteland that was one of the last places to lose its ice at the close of the Ice Age. The final approach is heralded by the Buachaille Etive Mor, one of Scotland's most imposing mountains.

RECOMMENDED WALKS

Near Glen Coe, there are interesting stretches of the West Highland Way, such as the Devil's Staircase. The Lost Valley in Glen Coe is another good walk, but needs a bit of scrambling experience. Advice on walks in Glen Coe can be obtained from the NTS Visitor Centre.

The visitor centre near the foot of the glen has displays on the district and tells one of Scotland's most tragic stories, the Glencoe Massacre of February 1692. In 1691 William III offered a pardon to the warring clans on condition that they took an oath of allegiance to the crown by 1 January 1692. The local MacDonald chief reluctantly made his way to Fort William just before the deadline in order to take the oath, only to be told that he should go to Inveraray. He did so, but arrived there a day after the deadline had passed. The regiment in Glen Coe at that time was under the command of a Campbell and they were billeted with the MacDonalds for 10 days. A message was sent to them, which had the King's private approval, and at a given signal, without warning, the Campbells rose up and slaughtered 38 of their hosts, supposedly because of the failure to take the oath. About 300 people escaped into the hills, but the atrocity was never forgotten.

i *NTS Visitor Centre (seasonal)*

▶ *Continue on the A82 past the village of Glencoe to Ballachulish.*

Golden sunset silhouetting romantic Castle Stalker

⑩ Ballachulish, Highland
This was once Scotland's main slate producer and in the 1880s, the quarries' peak of production, 600 men produced 16 million slates a year. This ended in 1955 but the massive quarries can still be seen behind the houses. The tourist information centre has an interesting display on the life and work of the quarries.

Steps under the Ballachulish Bridge, lead to a memorial to James Stewart who was hanged here in 1752 for the murder of Colin Campbell, a government official. He was undoubtedly a scapegoat convicted by a partisan court and Robert Louis Stevenson used this terrible miscarriage of justice in his novel *Kidnapped.*

i *Ballachulish (seasonal)*

▶ *Continue on the A82, then follow the A828 to the village of Portnacroish for Castle Stalker.*

⑪ Castle Stalker, Strathclyde
This romantically set rectangular keep is perched on a low rocky platform at the mouth of Loch Laich. It was built by the

Feeding the seals at the Sea Life Centre in Oban

Stewarts of Appin in the 13th century and in 1689, when it was in the possession of the Stewarts, it was exchanged for a meagre eight-oared galley during a drunken spree when the owner was not in full control of his senses!

▶ *Continue on the **A828** for 13 miles (21km) to the Oban Sea Life Centre, near Barcardine.*

🔟 **Oban Sea Life Centre,** Strathclyde

Scotland's west coast is famous for its important fishing grounds so it is entirely appropriate to have the Sea Life Centre here. Crabs, lobsters, rays and a huge shoal of herring are just some of the exhibits on view. There are also seals and it provides sanctuary to abandoned seal pups. Make sure you are there for one of the feeding times.

▶ *Continue on the **A828** to Connel where the road crosses the mouth of Loch Etive, 6 miles (10km).*

Fishing boats, car ferries and yachts make Oban one of the busiest harbours in Scotland

🔟 **Loch Etive,** Strathclyde

Just under the Connel Bridge are the unusual Falls of Lora, a tidal waterfall where the direction of the falls depends on whether the tide is going in or out. To the east stands the village of Taynuilt. This was once one of Scotland's iron smelting centres and the impressive Bonawe Furnace has been conserved to show something of what an 18th-century ironworks looked like; however, you will have to forget the peace and quiet of the countryside to imagine all the dust, dirt and smoke it must have once produced.

▶ *At Connel, join the **A85** and return to Oban.*

'Doon
the Watter'

The town of Paisley grew up around its abbey, founded in 1163, and is best known for its shawls featuring the distinctive teardrop-shaped Paisley pattern. From Paisley the tour explores the sea lochs and green-clad mountains of the

2 DAYS • 213KM • 132 MILES Cowal Peninsula.

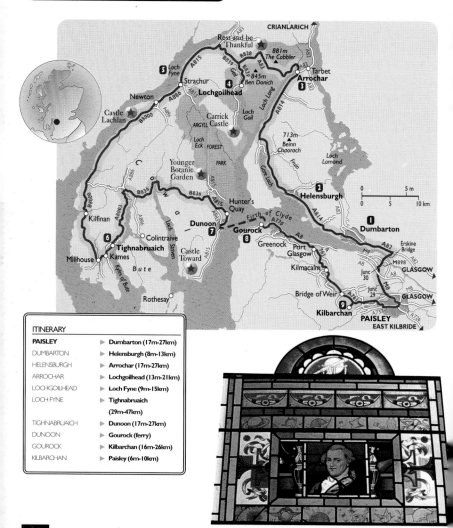

ITINERARY

PAISLEY	▶ **Dumbarton** (17m-27km)
DUMBARTON	▶ **Helensburgh** (8m-13km)
HELENSBURGH	▶ **Arrochar** (17m-27km)
ARROCHAR	▶ **Lochgoilhead** (13m-21km)
LOCHGOILHEAD	▶ **Loch Fyne** (9m-15km)
LOCH FYNE	▶ **Tighnabruaich** (29m-47km)
TIGHNABRUAICH	▶ **Dunoon** (17m-27km)
DUNOON	▶ **Gourock** (ferry)
GOUROCK	▶ **Kilbarchan** (16m-26km)
KILBARCHAN	▶ **Paisley** (6m-10km)

$\boxed{i}$ *Lagoon Centre, Mill street (seasonal)*

▶ *Leave Paisley on the **A726** (to Greenock and Erskine Bridge). Join the **M8** and head towards Greenock, then take the **M898/A898** to the Erskine Bridge (toll) over the River Clyde. Head west along the **A82** (towards Crianlarich) then bear left on to the **A814**.*

❶ Dumbarton, Strathclyde
A modern industrial town owing its historic importance to its prominent position on the northern shore of the River Clyde, Dumbarton was the capital of the ancient kingdom of Strathclyde and it has had a royal castle since medieval times. Dumbarton Castle stands on Dumbarton Rock overlooking the river and much of the present fortification dates from the 16th to 18th centuries. The hilltop behind the castle gives a superb view of the area.

Dumbarton is now an important whisky distilling

The river port of Dumbarton, now more famous for its whisky distilling than for its shipbuilding

centre but it used to have a flourishing shipbuilding industry. Although few ships are built on the Clyde these days, one important structure that remains is the Denny Tank which has been preserved by the Scottish Maritime Museum. This was used for experiments; models of proposed ships were towed along the 330-foot (100m) tank in order to show how the full size ship might perform at sea.

$\boxed{i}$ *Milton A82 north-bound*

Dumbarton Castle, situated on a hilltop overlooking the River Clyde

▶ *Leave Dumbarton by the **A814** and follow it along the coast for 8 miles (13km) to Helensburgh.*

Climbing up Glen Croe to 'Rest and be Thankful'

2 **Helensburgh,** Strathclyde

Helensburgh's grand architecture dates back to the late 18th century when it was built as a planned dormitory town for Glasgow, to which it was connected by regular sailings. The town's long promenade gives a pleasant walk and by the seafront is a tall granite obelisk commemorating Henry Bell, designer of the world's first sea-going steamship, *The Comet*.

The recent revival in interest in the work of the outstanding Scottish architect and designer Charles Rennie Mackintosh makes a trip to Hill House one of the town's main attractions. This mansion was built at the beginning of the 20th century for the publisher Walter Blackie and remains an outstanding example of modern Scottish domestic architecture. The exterior design and the household furnishings reflect Mackintosh's individual style.

John Logie Baird, pioneer of television, came from Helensburgh and a memorial bust to him is in the town's Hermitage Park.

After leaving Helensburgh, the route passes the huge complex of the Clyde Submarine Base.

i Clock Tower, The Pier (seasonal)

▶ *Continue along the **A814** for 17 miles (27km) to Arrochar.*

4 **Arrochar,** Strathclyde

The little village of Arrochar sits at the head of Loch Long and below the hills often referred to as the 'Arrochar Alps'. These rise steeply from the shore and provide wonderful walking and climbing, especially 2,891-foot (881m) Ben Arthur, which is usually known as The Cobbler.

Loch Long has been associated with seafarers for many centuries. The most notable naval exploit was in 1263 when the Viking King Haakon landed at Arrochar. He had his boats hauled 1½ miles (2km) over the strip of land to Tarbet and then sailed over Loch Lomond to attack inland settlements!

To the west of Arrochar, the A83 climbs steeply up Glen Croe to the well-named 'Rest and be Thankful' inn, which is at an altitude of 803 feet (245m). Below this can be seen the earlier military road which was built after the 1745 Jacobite uprising in order to 'pacify' the Highlands.

i *Pier Road, Tarbet (Seasonal)*

RECOMMENDED WALKS

Experienced walkers will head for the Arrocher Alps, but there are other walks of varying grades in the Argyll Forest Park which lies in the area of lochs Long, Goil and Eck. Information can be obtained from tourist information centres.

Taking the easy route up to 'Rest and be Thankful'

▷ *Leave Arrochar on the **A83** to Campbeltown. Turn left at the 'Rest and be Thankful' on to the **B828**, then join the **B839** to reach Lochgoilhead.*

❹ Lochgoilhead

Set at the head of Loch Goil, this village is popular with visitors seeking good walking and sailing. Beside the village is the European Sheep and Wool Centre, part of a leisure complex that offers various sports, including curling in the winter.

Five miles (8km) down the western shore of the loch stands the ruin of Carrick Castle, destroyed by fire in 1685. The structure dates at least from the 15th century and was probably used by James IV when he came to this area, known as Cowal, to hunt wild boar.

▷ *Leave Lochgoilhead by the **B839** and follow this to the shore of Loch Fyne. Turn left on to the **A815** just before the shore.*

❺ Loch Fyne, Strathclyde

This long sea loch is set among beautiful ranges of green-clad mountains. Apart from the little village of Strachur, the district's settlements are small and scattered and many of the houses are used as retirement homes.

South of Strachur stands Castle Lachlan, home of the chief of the MacLachlans. During the Clearances the local people were moved out of their homes and settled in the village of Newton which the chief built between the castle and Strachur. This is now a sleepy hamlet, and many homes are used only at weekends. The 18th-century Clearances, when landowners moved thousands of people off the land to make way for more profitable sheep farming, led to depopulation of the area. However, the importance of sheep has diminished greatly and much of the poorer land has

---

BACK TO NATURE

The sea lochs around Cowal are home to many seabirds including gulls, cormorants and ducks. Keep a sharp look out for seals from the shore of Loch Fyne. Of all Cowal's lochs, Loch Striven is probably the quietest and least touched by agriculture.

---

been given over to extensive conifer plantations.

▷ *Follow the **A815** to Strachur. Keep to the lochside by joining the **A886** and later bear right on to the **B8000** to Kilfinan. Follow this to Tighnabruaich.*

❻ Tighnabruaich,
Strathclyde

Both Tighnabruaich and neighbouring Kames grew during the heyday of steamship navigation on the Clyde. This is a popular sailing centre and many yachts can be seen in the narrow waterways around the northern coast of Bute. Just north of Tighnabruaich is one of Scotland's most famous viewpoints – across the narrow strait known as the Kyles of Bute.

FOR CHILDREN

Cowal is an area for outdoor activites with sailing at Tighnabruaich and pony-trekking at Lochgoilhead and Inellan (south of Dunoon). As a wet-weather alternative, there are swimming pools in Dunoon and Lochgoilhead.

▷ *Leave Tighnabruaich by the **A8003**. Turn right at the **A886** and then left at the **B836**. Turn right on the **A815** for Dunoon.*

❼ Dunoon, Strathclyde

Dunoon has built up a reputation as one of the most popular stopping places for people sailing 'Doon the Watter', as the Glaswegians say, and its picturesque pierhead buildings have welcomed countless visitors. As befits a seaside resort, it has a long promenade and colourful Castle Gardens.

Near the pier stands a statue of Robert Burns' 'Highland Mary' who was born in the town. This was Mary Campbell, who was betrothed to Burns but died. Burns tried hard to cover up their relationship, probably because it complicated his life with his future wife, Jean Armour. A castle, which was razed in 1685, stood on the high ground behind the statue and this viewpoint provides a fine outlook over the busy Clyde.

Dunoon is world famous for its Cowal Highland Gathering which takes place on the last Friday and Saturday in August. The Gathering was started in the 1890s and today it attracts competitors from many coun-

Younger Botanic Gardens – woodland gardens on a grand scale

tries as it hosts World Championship highland dancing. Pipe bands from near and far compete at the Gathering and some 20,000 visitors hve been known to throng the main street watching the bands marching through the town.

The Younger Botanic Garden is at Benmore, just 7

miles (11km) north of Dunoon on the A815. This outstanding garden is an outstation of

FOR HISTORY BUFFS

Eight miles (13km) south of Dunoon stand the ruins of 15th-century Castle Toward. This was a stronghold of the Lamont clan, but in 1646 it was surrounded by a force of Campbells. Although the Lamonts accepted and signed a truce they were seized and taken to Dunoon where they were summarily executed and their bodies thrown into mass graves. This bloody act is commemorated by a memorial on Tom-a-Mhoid Road near Castle Hill.

SPECIAL TO ...

The development of steamships in the 19th century led to the 'discovery' of Cowal by visitors keen to go 'Doon the Watter' (the River Clyde) from Glasgow to the smoke-free countryside. Many wealthy Glasgow merchants built villas in the Cowal villages and decanted their families there during the summer months. Cruising on the Clyde is now an increasingly popular pastime and cruises from places such as Dunoon and Tighnabruaich are available. One ship to look out for around Cowal is the *PS Waverley*, the world's last sea-going paddle steamer. It is based in Glasgow and operates many summer cruises, calling at piers on both sides of the Firth of Clyde.

Edinburgh's Royal Botanic Garden; it has a magnificent collection of rhododendrons and an impressive avenue of tall redwoods that was planted here in 1863.

ℹ️ *7 Alexandra Parade*

▶ *Take the Caledonian MacBrayne ferry from Dunoon to Gourock. Alternatively, take the Western Ferries' ferry from Hunter's Quay (just north of Dunoon) to a point a little southwest of Gourock; then head towards Gourock on the A770.*

8 Gourock, Strathclyde
Gourock is a pleasant coastal town that boasts excellent views of the Clyde. Perhaps the best view is from Lyle Hill which stands above the southeastern side of Gourock Bay. On top of the hill is a monument in the form of a Cross of Lorraine commemorating Free French sailors who sailed from here and died during World War II's Battle of the Atlantic.

To the east of Gourock are the industrial towns of Greenock and Port Glasgow. Greenock was a shipbuilding centre and once an important embarkation point for emigrants leaving Scotland for new lives in North America or Australasia. The town's most famous son was the engineer James Watt, whose invention of the condensing steam engine, the first efficient use of steam power, paved the way for the Industrial Revolution. The notorious privateer and pirate Captain Kidd may also have come from Greenock, but would any town want to claim him as one of their own?

Port Glasgow gained its present name in 1688 when it became the city's port as ships could not progress further upstream (its previous name had been Newark). The city's 16th-century castle still stands by the shore, although it is rather overshadowed these days by the many industrial buildings all around it.

▶ *Leave Gourock by the coastal road (the A770 which joins the A8 at Greenock) and bear right on to the A761 to Bridge of Weir, via Kilmacolm. After Bridge of Weir, continue on the A761 for 1½ miles (2.5km) after the local railway station, then turn sharp right at a signposted minor road to Kilbarchan.*

9 Kilbarchan, Strathclyde
In the 18th century the village of Kilbarchan was an important centre where wool, linen and cotton were hand woven. A weaver's cottage of 1723 has been preserved at The Cross by the NTS. This continued to be used for weaving until 1940 and it has a 200-year-old loom on which weaving demonstrations are now given.

Hand-woven tartans are still made today at Kilbarchan

▶ *Rejoin the A761 (to Paisley, via Linwood), then turn left on to the A737 to return to Paisley.*

SCENIC ROUTES

The nicest part of this tour is on the A8003, when the narrows of the Kyles of Bute are seen. If you are lucky you may see a ship negotiating the passage past the Burnt Islands. The true narows are opposite Colintraive, whose name means 'straight of swimming', dating from the times when cattle drovers used to swim their beasts across here.

Rob Roy
Country

WASHING THE FLEECE

This tour takes in two of Scotland's most famous lochs – Loch Lomond and Loch Tay – but starts in Glasgow, one of Britain's most exciting cities. It is certainly worth spending a few days in Glasgow: its museums and galleries are among Britain's finest and the city is well endowed with green spaces.

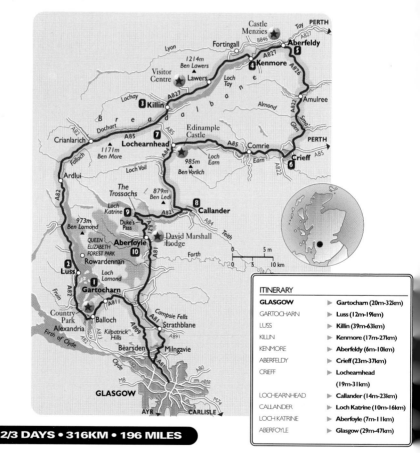

ITINERARY

GLASGOW	▶	**Gartocharn (20m-32km)**
GARTOCHARN	▶	**Luss (12m-19km)**
LUSS	▶	**Killin (39m-63km)**
KILLIN	▶	**Kenmore (17m-27km)**
KENMORE	▶	**Aberfeldy (6m-10km)**
ABERFELDY	▶	**Crieff (23m-37km)**
CRIEFF	▶	**Lochearnhead**
		(19m-31km)
LOCHEARNHEAD	▶	**Callander (14m-23km)**
CALLANDER	▶	**Loch Katrine (10m-16km)**
LOCH KATRINE	▶	**Aberfoyle (7m-11km)**
ABERFOYLE	▶	**Glasgow (29m-47km)**

2/3 DAYS • 316KM • 196 MILES

▶ *Leave by the **A81**, then the **A809** and turn left at the **A811** to reach Gartocharn.*

❶ Gartocharn, Strathclyde
This small village gives a good introduction to Scotland's most-loved loch, Loch Lomond. Although Gartocharn doesn't actually sit on the lochside, there is a superb view of it from the hill behind, Duncryne. For little effort, this is a vantage point that gives views towards the loch, 3,194-foot (974m) Ben Lomond on the east shore and the Luss Hills, which rise from the western shore.
    The area around the loch was one of the last places to lose its glaciers at the end of the Ice Age and the smooth, U-shaped glacial valleys in the Luss Hills are obvious features of this type of landscape. The careful observer will notice a change between this glacially-eroded highland landscape and the smoothly sculpted hillocks around Gartocharn's farmland. This change in scenery indicates the geological divide between the Highlands and the Lowlands.
    Further along the road, at Balloch, there are cruises available on the loch and pleasant walks in the Balloch Castle Country Park.

[i] *The Square, Drymen (seasonal)*

▶ *Continue on the **A811** and turn right at the **A82**. Follow this northwards, turning right at an unclassified road sign-posted to Luss, a distance of 12 miles (19km).*

❷ Luss, Strathclyde
The delightful little lochside village of Luss, has many

Contestant giving his best at the World Pipe Band Championships in Glasgow

Majestic Loch Lomond as seen from Duncryne Hill

exceptionally picturesque cottages. The Loch Lomond Park Visitor Centre is located here, and the Thistle Bagpipe Works are nearby. Further north, a ferry operates from Inverbeg across the loch to Rowardennan.

Kenmore church and boats on Loch Tay

RECOMMENDED WALKS

Hillwalkers will find plenty of good hills near a number of villages. Crainlarich has two interesting pairs of hills in Beinn a' Chroin and Beinn Tulaichean, and Ben More and Stob Binnein. Killin has Ben Lawers and the group of hills called the Tarmachans. Lower hills further south include Ben Venue, Ben Ledi and Ben An. The forests, especially around Aberfoyle, offer many walks, though views of the hills and lochs may be restricted at times by the trees. The David Marshall Lodge at Aberfoyle is run by the Forestry Commission and many marked paths start from here. Other walks include parts of the West Highland Way (which follows the eastern shore of Loch Lomond), to the Bracklinn Falls (near Callander) and to the Falls of Moness (near Aberfeldy).

▶ *Rejoin and continue on the A82, then turn right on to the A85 at Crianlarich. Turn left at the A827 to Killin (39 miles/63km).*

BACK TO NATURE

The rich flora on Ben Lawers attracts many botanists, both amateur and professional, to this remarkable mountain. The hill is rich in lime and other minerals which provide the nutrients needed by the Arctic/Alpine species that grow here. Cliff edges, which are out of reach of sheep and deer, support such plants as roseroot, angelica and wood cranesbill, while shady crevices host oak fern and wood anemone. Birds are not too common on the higher slopes but look out for buzzards and kestrels, with occasional sightings of golden eagles and peregrines. Mountain hares can be seen on the high ground.

3 Killin, Central
Killin is a popular centre with hill walkers as there are so many fine hills in the district, the best known of which is Ben Lawers, at 3,984 feet (1,214m). The NTS has established a visitor centre on the western flank of the mountain.

The River Dochart flows past the village before debouching into Loch Tay. Before reaching the village it tumbles over the wide Falls of Dochart, which are quite fearsome when the river is in spate.

i *Breadalbane Folklore Centre (seasonal)*

▶ *Continue on the A827 for 17 miles (27km) to Kenmore.*

4 Kenmore, Tayside
On the shores of Loch Tay, Kenmore has been developed as a small resort and watersports centre. Beside the village is the ornamental gateway to 19th-century Taymouth Castle

SCENIC ROUTES

Much of the route is through fine scenery, with perhaps the best parts being along the shores of lochs Lomond and Tay for views of the lochs and their mountains.
Another fine stretch is through the pretty Sma'Glen (between Aberfeldy and Crieff) where the River Almond winds its way through the hills.

(private), which stands in fine parkland, part of which is now used as a golf course.

To the north lies the quiet settlement of Fortingall, reputedly the birthplace of Pontius Pilate, which had several roadside thatched cottages. A yew tree in the churchyard is said to be over 3000 years old.

▶ *Continue on the A827 for 6 miles (10km) to Aberfeldy.*

5 Aberfeldy, Tayside

This pleasant touring centre stands beside the splendidly ornate bridge which General George Wade built in 1733 at this important crossing of the River Tay. Wade was responsible

for some 250 miles (400km) of military roads in the Highlands between 1726 and 1735, as part of the Government's attempt to gain control over the region. This network included 40 stone bridges, of which this is the best known, and at the time it was the only bridge over the Tay. The Black Watch Memorial, which stands quite close to the bridge, was erected in 1887. The regiment was enrolled into the British Army in 1739 and took its name from the men's dark tartan, chosen to differentiate them from the Guardsmen or Red Soldiers.

Aberfeldy lies in a belt of good agricultural land and the water mill is one enduring reminder of how the local grain was processed. This was originally built in 1825 and has been restored to allow it to produce stoneground oatmeal. To the northwest of the village, at Weem, stands Castle Menzies, home of the chief of Clan Menzies. The present castle, Z-shaped in plan, was built in the 1570s, and has been restored by the Clan Society.

i *The Square*

▶ *Leave by the A826. Turn right at the A822, then right at the A85 and follow this into Crieff.*

6 Crieff, Tayside

Crieff is a traditional Highland resort and one that offers much to the visitor wanting a base to explore the countryside. Perthshire Paperweights and Thistle Pottery have a visitor centre and offer factory tours. The local Glenturret Distillery, founded in 1775, has a visitor centre and tours round the premises. West of Crieff, on the A85, is Comrie, a pretty village surrounded by wooded crags.

i *High Street*

▶ *Continue on the A85 for 19 miles (31km) to Lochearnhead.*

7 Lochearnhead, Central

Lochearnhead, at the western end of Loch Earn, was developed when the railway was built through Glen Ogle. The line's route can be followed through the glen and look out for the massive boulders that have tumbled down the hillside and must have threatened the trains that chugged up the steep incline. Near the village, where the Burn of Ample meets the loch, stands Edinample Castle which was built in 1630.

Crieff's local Glenturret Distillery

▶ *Leave by the A84 and follow it for 14 miles (23km) to Callander.*

8 Callander, Central

This is one of Central Scotland's busiest little resorts as it is a favourite stopping place for many visitors.

The town stands by the banks of the River Teith and has many good walks near by.

Serious walkers head for Ben Ledi, which dominates the local scenery at 2,882 feet (879m), or the rather higher Ben Vorlich, at 3,231 feet (985m) which stands between Callander town and Loch Earn.

Much of the town was laid out in the 18th century as a planned village with its centre at Ancaster Square which now houses the Rob Roy and Trossachs Visitor Centre. Rob Roy MacGregor (1671–1734) was a most intriguing character and the hero of Sir Walter Scott's novel *Rob Roy*. The story of Rob Roy's life is intertwined with legend and Scott's artistic licence. However, he did represent the last flings of Gaeldom against the encroaching 'civilisation' of the Highlands by English and lowland Scottish 'culture' as well as naked economic and political might. At the end of the 17th century the king, William of Orange, was determined to subdue the Highlanders and even took the step of proscribing the name MacGregor. Rob Roy then used his mother's clan name of Campbell and allied himself with his kinsman, the Duke of Argyll, in feuds with the Duke of Montrose. When Montrose chased him out of his home, he turned his hand from cattle

The summit of Ben Ledi, viewed from Duke's Pass

dealing to reiving (cattle raiding), earning a reputation as the Scots' equivalent of Robin Hood, stealing from the rich landowners and giving the money to destitute Highlanders.

i Ancaster Square (seasonal)

▶ *Return along the A84 and then turn left at the A821. After passing the Trossachs Hotel, follow the signs (right) to Loch Katrine.*

9 Loch Katrine, Central

The loch lies in the heart of the area known as the Trossachs, though the name is properly given to the little pass between lochs Achray and Katrine. Its fame as a beauty spot stemmed from Sir Walter Scott's description of it in the poem *The Lady of the Lake*; Dorothy Wordsworth and others also described its charms. The road between the loch and Aberfoyle is known as the Duke's Pass, as it was built in the 19th century by the Duke of Montrose to cater for the ever-increasing number of visitors coming to this part of the country, drawn here after reading Scott's work.

The loch is one of the main sources of Glasgow's water and the 1855 scheme to pipe this very pure water the 35 miles (56km) to the city was a massive feat of civil engineering. Today, visitors can cruise on the *Sir Walter Scott* across the waters of the loch and sail under the slopes of Ben Venue.

▶ *Return to the A821 and turn right. Follow the A821 to Aberfoyle, 7 miles (11km).*

10 Aberfoyle, Central

Aberfoyle is a tourist centre sitting by the River Forth and seemingly hemmed in by a very large conifer plantation, much of it within the Queen Elizabeth Forest Park. The 'Clachan at Aberfoyle' was one of the settings used by Scott in *Rob Roy*

Local attraction to be sampled at Aberfoyle

(a clachan is Scots for a small village). The village's Scottish Wool Centre features many different varieties of sheep bred in Scotland.

i Main Street (seasonal)

A steamer trip on the *Sir Walter Scott* provides a splendid view of Loch Katrine

▶ *Continue on the A821 and the A81. Follow this back to Glasgow, 29 miles (47km).*

FOR HISTORY BUFFS

To the east of Aberfoyle lies the Lake of Menteith, one of only a handful of 'lakes' in Scotland. On one of the lake's islands, Inchmahome, stands the Priory of Inchmahome, founded in 1238. Mary, Queen of Scots, was sent to the island at the age of five, prior to sailing to France in 1547. The island can be reached by ferry from the Port of Menteith.

TOUR 11

Abbeys,
Battlefields & Castles

This tour covers many of the historic sights which make up Scotland's bloody history. Strategically positioned on the eastern route into the Highlands, Stirling saw two great battles during the Wars of Independence – in 1297 at Stirling Bridge and in 1314 at Bannockburn.

1/2 DAYS • 148KM • 91 MILES

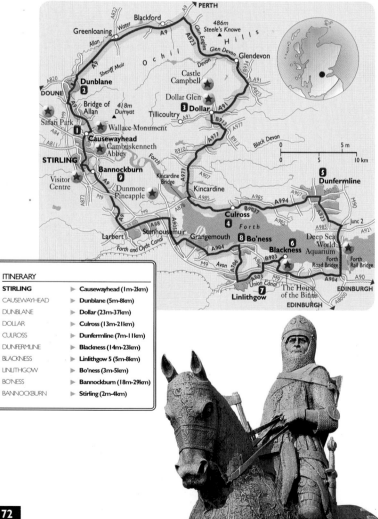

ITINERARY

STIRLING	▶ **Causewayhead** (1m-2km)
CAUSEWAYHEAD	▶ **Dunblane** (5m-8km)
DUNBLANE	▶ **Dollar** (23m-37km)
DOLLAR	▶ **Culross** (13m-21km)
CULROSS	▶ **Dunfermline** (7m-11km)
DUNFERMLINE	▶ **Blackness** (14m-23km)
BLACKNESS	▶ **Linlithgow 5** (5m-8km)
LINLITHGOW	▶ **Bo'ness** (3m-5km)
BO'NESS	▶ **Bannockburn** (18m-29km)
BANNOCKBURN	▶ **Stirling** (2m-4km)

i 41 Dumbarton Road; Castle
Esplanade; M9/M80 Junction 9
Motorway Service Area
(seasonal)

FOR CHILDREN

The Blair Drummond Safari
and Leisure Park is to be found
to the northwest of Stirling, on
the flat agricultural land of the
Carse of Stirling. The most
fascinating part of the park is
the drive round the main
enclosure, where you can
observe wild animals such as
lions, zebra and deer, roaming
around at very close quarters;
don't be surprised if you find
there are monkeys clambering
all over your car!

▶ Leave by the **A9** and follow it
for 1 mile (2km) to
Causewayhead.

❶ Causewayhead, Central
This small village is dominated
by the Abbey Craig upon which
is perched the 220-foot (67m)
high Wallace Monument,
erected in tribute to Sir William
Wallace, victor of the Battle of
Stirling Bridge. The top of the

monument gives an outstanding
view of the district. Close to the
village in a meander of the
Forth stands the ruined
Cambuskenneth Abbey,
founded around 1147.

▶ Continue on the **A9**. Just
before Dunblane, turn right at
a roundabout at the end of
the **M9** and follow the
B8033. Take a
signposted road
on the left into the
village, 5 miles
(8km).

❷ Dunblane,
Central
The cathedral, which
is situated near Allan
Water, was founded
around 1150 and its
presence raises the
status of the village to
that of a small city.
To the west lies the
quiet village of
Doune. Its main
attractions today
are the fine medieval
castle and the

Costume pageant at
the Queen Mary
Gardens, Stirling Castle

Panoramic view of the ramparts of
Stirling Castle and the Church of
the Holy Rude.

collection of rare vehicles in the
Motor Museum, including the
world's second oldest Rolls
Royce.

i Stirling Road, Dunblane
(seasonal)

[i] Mill Trail Visitor Centre, Alva

▶ Leave by the **B913** and turn right at the **A977**. Turn right at the **A876**, heading towards Kincardine Bridge, turn left just before and follow an unclassified road along the coast to Culross.

4 Culross, Fife

Culross, frozen in time, is possibly Scotland's most remarkable town. During the 16th and 17th centuries, it prospered by trading in coal and salt with ports across the North Sea, but when this failed, the town declined. Fortunately it never really changed during the industrial development of the succeeding centuries, so although it is quite small it preserves many of the features that have been lost in other ancient towns. The NTS has played a major part in conserving this unique place, especially through its 'Little Houses Scheme', and today numerous buildings can be visited, whisking you back through the centuries. Cobbled streets and white-painted buildings with pantile roofs help to produce an air that is so very different from any other Scottish town and the virtual completeness of the medieval character of Culross has attracted many television and film companies to locations here.

The town's main building, the Palace, was never in fact a royal mansion at all, but the home of the local laird, George Bruce, and was originally built between 1597 and 1611. The title deeds describe it as 'the Palace of Great Lodging in the Sand Haven of Culross'. Among the other fascinating buildings here, visitors should look out for the Town House, the Study, the House of the Evil Eye and the abbey.

Bird's-eye view of the impressive stronghold of Castle Campbell, Dollar

SCENIC ROUTES

The journey through Glen Eagles and Glen Devon is the most scenic part of the tour, with the road making its way through the heart of the Ochils. Two misconceptions about Glen Eagles should be explained; firstly, the name means 'churches' and not 'eagles' and secondly, the golfing hotel of Gleneagles is not here but near Auchterarder.

▶ Return to the **B8033** and turn left. Join the **A9** and head towards Perth. Turn right at the **A823**, then right at the **A91** in order to enter Dollar.

3 Dollar, Central

This neat little town lies in a sheltered position at the foot of the Ochil Hills and one of its chief attractions is the wooded Dollar Glen, through which a path runs to Castle Campbell. This stands on a promontory overlooking the confluence of two streams, intriguingly named the Burn of Sorrow and the Burn of Care. Until 1490 it was called Castle Glume, hence it is sometimes referred to as the 'castle of gloom'.

Dollar is one of the Hillfoot towns, small mill towns which gained prosperity through the woollen industry. A mill trail links these communities and guides visitors through the district. Tillicoultry's Clock Mill Heritage Centre is the focal point of this trail and it has displays explaining the history of the local woollen industry.

▶ Continue on the unclassified road, then turn right at the **B9037**. Join the **A994** which leads to Dunfermline (7 miles/11km).

5 Dunfermline, Fife

Dunfermline was built around a substantial Benedictine abbey which was constructed in the 12th century. Apart from the abbey church, there are the ruins of the monastery's domestic buildings and the palace, which was often used as the abbey's guest house. The abbey church was a favoured place with the Scottish kings and it superseded Iona as their place of burial. The great warrior, King Robert the Bruce, was buried here but it was only in 1818 that this fact was known for certain. During some restoration work, a skeleton, dressed in what may have been royal robes, was discovered and it was noticed that the breast bone had been sawn in order to remove one of the organs. This would have been in accordance with Bruce's deathbed wish in 1329 that upon his death his heart be removed and taken to the Holy Land as his way of making up for not taking part in the Crusades. His heart was buried in Melrose Abbey. Abbot House was the administrative centre of the abbey and it now has a new lease of life as a museum depicting its use over the centuries. Opposite the door of the abbey church is the entrance to the extensive and pleasant Pittencrieff Park. Within the grounds is Pittencrieff House, built in the 17th century. There is a small museum of local history with an art gallery and a costume exhibition here.

The great fortress of Blackness Castle looking out over the North Sea

Just by the edge of the park stands the cottage where Andrew Carnegie was born in 1835. In 1848 his family emigrated to the US where he made his massive fortune in the steel industry. He then began to give much of his wealth away, buying Pittencrieff Park for the town and establishing trusts that endowed libraries and other public enterprises. The cottage is now the location of the Andrew Carnegie Birthplace Museum.

Detail of the plaque 'Discovery' at the Carnegie Birthplace Museum

$\boxed{i}$ 13–15 Maygate

▶ *Leave by the* **A823** *and the* **A823M**, *then join the* **M90** *to cross the Forth Road Bridge (toll). Turn right on to the* **A904**, *then right along the* **B903** *to Blackness (14 miles/23 km).*

6 Blackness, Lothian

The little village of Blackness, once an important seaport, is dominated by the great fortress of Blackness Castle. This was built to protect the port which was the harbour for the great royal palace at Linlithgow. Construction of the castle started as a fairly small affair in the 15th century, but with later technical improvements in artillery it became necessary to strengthen it to withstand massive sea-borne attacks. After the Union with England in 1707, it was one of the four castles in Scotland allowed to be left fortified.

▶ *Return until the* **A904** *is met. Turn left on to the* **A904** *and then follow the* **A803** *to Linlithgow.*

7 Linlithgow, Lothian

The history of the town is intimately interwoven with that of the palace, the birthplace of Mary, Queen of Scots, and one of the country's most important historical buildings. There was some form of royal residence here in the 14th century, but the present palace was not started until the early 16th century. It was certainly a substantial and well-defended building, occupying an attractive site overlooking Linlithgow Loch. Everything seems to have been constructed to a grand scale, especially the enormous fireplaces and the ornate fountain that stands in the quadrangle in the heart of the building.

Linlithgow has a number of other fine buildings and monuments sited near the palace or on the main street and these include the Church of St Michael, the Burgh Halls, the House of the Binns and the Cross Well. The story of the town is told in the Linlithgow Heritage Centre.

The Union Canal, which joined the Forth and Clyde Canal to the heart of Edinburgh, runs along the town's outskirts.

This was originally built to bring coal from Lanarkshire into the capital. Work on the canal started in 1818 and it opened in 1822, finally closing in 1965. Today there is a canal museum at the Manse Road Basin and cruises are available.

i *Burgh Halls, The Cross*

▶ *Leave by the **A706** to Bo'ness.*

8 Bo'ness, Central

This long-established industrial town was once the third most important seaport in Scotland until the building of the Forth and Clyde Canal and the establishment of the major port at Grangemouth put it into decline. Bo'ness' past has included such diverse enterprises as potteries, salt pans, iron foundries and coal mines and it is most appropriate that the town's visitor facilities have taken advantage of this rich industrial legacy. It is possible to walk through the tunnels of the Birkhill Clay Mine. The Bo'ness and Kinneil Railway operates steam trains on its 3½-mile (6km) track that runs along the foreshore.

Interior of the House of Binns, Linlithgow, the historic home of the Dalyell family

i *Union Street*

▶ *Leave by the **A904** and turn right at the **A905**. Turn left at the **A88** and right at the **A9**. Continue on this road towards Stirling and turn left at the **A872** to reach the NTS Visitor Centre at Bannockburn.*

One of the old trains on Bo'ness' steam railway

9 Bannockburn, Central
The Battle of Bannockburn in 1314 was one of the most important events in the fight for Scottish independence. At the time, an English force held Stirling Castle and was being besieged by Robert the Bruce's brother. The English army, led by their king, came north to relieve the castle and a pitched battle took place here. The Scots army, led by Bruce, eventually routed the enemy after they took fright at seeing a 'new' army (in reality, the Scots camp followers) come over the Gillies Hill. The story of the battle and the history of that period is explained in the NTS's Visitor Centre and the impressive memorial to the battle is in the form of a bronze equestrian statue of Bruce erected where his command post is thought to have been positioned.

[i] *NTS Visitor Centre*

▶ *Return along the **A872** and turn left at the **B8051** to Stirling.*

A dramatic view of the Forth Rail Bridge

Raspberry Fields
Forever

1/2 DAYS • 192KM • 120 MILES

The land circling the Sidlaw Hills is an area often overlooked by tourists, yet it has much to offer in terms of pretty coastal villages and green, gentle countryside. The renowned 'Fair City' of Perth is the chief town of this important farming region, and is located in a most attractive setting beside the River Tay.

ITINERARY	
PERTH	➤ **Dunkeld (15m-24km)**
DUNKELD	➤ **Blairgowrie (11m-18km)**
BLAIRGOWRIE	➤ **Meigle (8m-13km)**
MEIGLE	➤ **Glamis (7m-11km)**
GLAMIS	➤ **Brechin (17m-27km)**
BRECHIN	➤ **House of Duns (5m-8km)**
HOUSE OF DUNS	➤ **SMontrose (4m-6km)**
MONTROSE	➤ **Arbroath (13m-21km)**
ARBROATH	➤ **Carnoustie (7m-11km)**
CARNOUSTIE	➤ **Dundee (11m-18km)**
DUNDEE	➤ **Perth (22m-35km)**

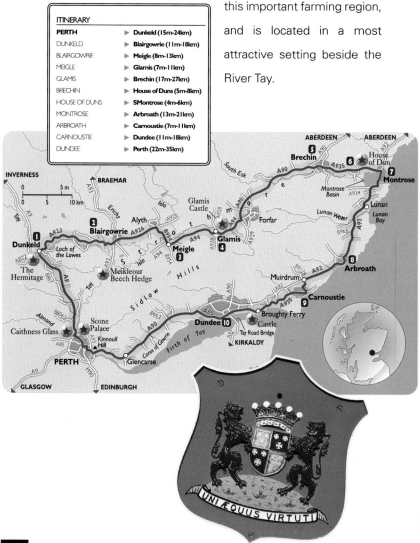

i *45 High Street, Perth; Caithness Glass Car Park, Inveralmond, by the A9 (seasonal)*

▶ *Leave by the A912 and join the A9 (to Inverness). Turn right at the A923 and follow this into Dunkeld (15 miles/24km).*

◘ Dunkeld, Tayside

The history of Dunkeld goes back to Pictish times but the town's importance in Scottish history is as Kenneth MacAlpin's ecclesiastical capital in the 9th century. This eventually led to the construction, in the early 14th century, of the cathedral which stands by the banks of the River Tay. Although much of it is roofless, the choir was restored and within it is the tomb of Alexander Stewart, the notorious 'Wolf of Badenoch'.

In the centre of Dunkeld stands a very ornate fountain and between this and the cathedral are the Little Houses, which were built in the late 17th century. Look out for the NTS's The Ell Shop on whose wall is an original ell measure, a little over a metre long, which was used for measuring cloth. Beside

it is The Duchess Anne, formerly a school, which houses the cathedral art exhibition each summer.

i *The Cross (seasonal*

FOR HISTORY BUFFS

Perth became important when Scotland's first king, Kenneth MacAlpin, took the legendary Stone of Destiny to Scone Palace which lies just to the north of the town. Legend has it that this was the Biblical Jacob's pillow and it became the 'throne' upon which Scottish kings were crowned. In 1296, Edward I (the 'Hammer of the Scots') removed this symbol of Scottish nationhood to London's Westminster Abbey, but on Christmas Eve in 1950 the stone was taken by a small group of Scots. It 'disappeared' until 1952, when the stone was recovered at Arbroath Abbey (whether or not it was the original stone remains unresolved), and in 1997 it was finally returned to the Scots.

RECOMMENDED WALKS

Kinnoull Hill, about a mile (1.5km) from the centre of Perth, offers an outstanding view over the surrounding countryside. The Hermitage near Dunkeld is the site of a woodland walk in the care of the NTS. Two interesting follies and a waterfall make a stroll here a pleasant outing.

BACK TO NATURE

The Loch of the Lowies lies to the east of Dunkeld and there are plenty of hides from which it is possible to see many birds, including ospreys and Slavonian grebes in the summer. In winter, look out for greylag geese, pochards and goldeneye.

▶ *Continue on the A923 and follow it for 11 miles (18km) to Blairgowrie.*

Detail from the window above the altar in Dunkeld Cathedral

Raspberry Fields Forever

The wonderfully ornate Glamis Castle, childhood home of the Queen Mother

A bustling little town, Blairgowrie is well situated as a touring centre, lying at the junction of five roads. The district's most remarkable feature is just 5 miles (8km) to the south on the A93: the magnificent Meikleour Beech Hedge. This was originally planted in 1746 and is now some 110 feet (33m) high and 2,000 feet (600m) long. It is trimmed once every 10 years.

☐ *26 Wellmeadow*

▶ *Leave by the A926 then turn right at the B954 to Meigle.*

3 Meigle, Tayside
For such a small village, the local museum has a remarkable collection of carved stones. More than 30 significant stones have been found in the area and these portray ancient symbols such as Pictish beasts, a Persian god and a horseman. The dates vary, but most of them are from the 8th to 10th centuries.

To add further interest to the local history, the village may have had connections with King Arthur – his consort, Queen Guinevere, is believed to be buried here.

▶ *Leave by the A94 to approach Glamis, then take a minor road on the left to reach the village and the castle.*

4 Glamis, Tayside
Glamis Castle, the childhood home of the Queen Mother, and birthplace of Princess Margaret, is an excellent example of a large medieval tower house that has, over the centuries, been transformed into a palace. The long straight driveway leads directly up to its rather small entrance, an approach that seems to emphasise the symmetrical structure of the castle.

In comparison to the castle and its grand style of living, the village of Glamis houses the Angus Folk Collection. This occupies a row of 18th-century cottages and consists of rooms furnished as in bygone days. There are, for example, a kitchen, laundry, schoolhouse and a forge, all with appropriate equipment. Both museum and castle are closed in winter.

▶ *Continue on the A94, then turn left onto the A90. Bear right at the A935 to enter Brechin (17 miles/27km).*

5 Brechin, Tayside
The pleasant town of Brechin, with its many red sandstone buildings, lies in the heart of the rich agricultural area of Strathmore. Its most interesting feature is the tall, slim Round Tower, one of only two in Scotland. It dates from the 11th century and stands beside the remains of the 13th-century cathedral.

☐ *St Ninian's Place (seasonal)*

Continue on the **A935** and follow it for 5 miles (8km) to the House of Dun. (The driveway is to the left.)

6 House of Dun, Tayside
This 18th-century house was designed by William Adam, father of the Adam brothers who designed so many important buildings in Scotland. Recently restored by the NTS, it now reflects how it would have looked over 250 years ago with its public rooms featuring a wealth of exceptionally ornate baroque plasterwork.

Continue on the **A935**, then turn right at the **A92** for Montrose.

7 Montrose, Tayside
Montrose's wide main street lends an air of spaciousness to this seaside town. Its history, going back to the 10th century, owes much to the Montrose Basin which gave the town a uniquely strategic position on the east coast. It has been an important port for a long time and its economy has recently enjoyed a boost with the emergence of the North Sea oil industry. Of more interest to most visitors is the town's beach which is backed by sand dunes.

[i] Bridge Street (seasonal)

Continue on the **A92** and follow it to Arbroath.

FOR CHILDREN

The seaside resorts have good beaches but one 'remoter' stretch of sand can be found at the village of Lunan. The car-park at Lunan Bay's superb beach is reached by turning seawards just as the village is entered

8 Arbroath, Tayside
Arbroath is a busy seaside town which attracts many visitors each summer. It also has an active fishing industry and this is the home of the delicious 'Arbroath

smokie', a line-caught haddock that is smoke-cured using oak chips. The town's place in Scottish history was assured by the Declaration of Arbroath, a document drawn up in 1320 to state the independence of Scotland after the Battle of Bannockburn in 1314. The declaration was drawn up in the abbey, originally a priory founded in the 12th century.

[i] Market Place

Continue on the **A92**, then turn left at the **A930** to enter Carnoustie.

9 Carnoustie, Tayside
Carnoustie's fame as a resort is based on its extensive beach and the golf courses which lie on the sandy links. The championship courses have played host to the British and Scottish Open tournaments.

[i] The Library, High Street (seasonal)

Continue on the **A930** to Dundee.

10 Dundee, Tayside
The old saying that the industrial town of Dundee is famous for jute, jam and journalism is less correct these days as the town's prosperity is now based on a much broader spectrum of industries; the jute mills having been converted into luxury flats. Its coastal site has meant that the sea has always been of importance and many wooden ships for the whaling industry were built here. These ships had to withstand cruel polar conditions and this expertise was used in 1901 to build Captain Scott's ship *Discovery*, now berthed alongside the Discovery Point Visitor Centre. In the nearby Victoria Dock is the frigate *Unicorn*, built in 1825.

The city's history is told in the McManus Galleries, which also hold the local art collection; the Barrack Street Museum houses a natural history collection including the skeleton of a whale. The city's connections with the whaling industry are displayed in the 15th-century Broughty Castle Museum, by the Firth of Tay.

[i] 4 City Square

Leave by the **A85**, then turn left along the **A90** for the return to Perth.

SCENIC ROUTES

Hills are never very far away from much of this route and the views of the Sidlaw Hills and the foothills of the Grampian Mountains are good. On the drive to Dunkeld, it is interesting to note that the road is approaching a distinctive line of hills. These mark the geological boundary called the Highland Boundary Fault and indicate the 'real' start of the Scottish Highlands.

Scott's ship *Discovery*, berthed at Discovery Point

The Kingdom
of Fife

1/2 DAYS • 156KM • 97 MILES Surrounded by the Firths of Forth and Tay, the most important town in the Kingdom of Fife is undoubtedly St Andrews. Famous primarily for being the golfing capital of the world and home to the Royal & Ancient Golf Club, St Andrews is also the location of Britain's third oldest university after Oxford and Cambridge, founded in 1410. The rest of the region is dominated by pretty fishing villages and much land is given over to agriculture.

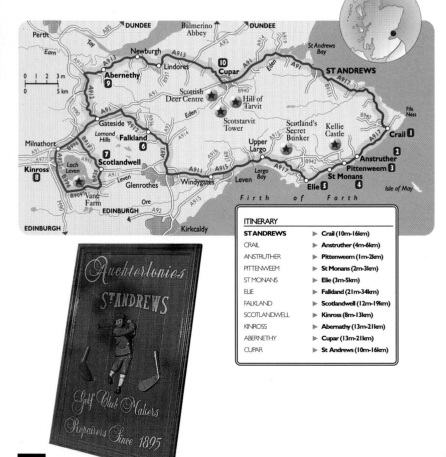

ITINERARY	
ST ANDREWS	► **Crail (10m-16km)**
CRAIL	► **Anstruther (4m-6km)**
ANSTRUTHER	► **Pittenweem (1m-2km)**
PITTENWEEM	► **St Monans (2m-3km)**
ST MONANS	► **Elie (3m-5km)**
ELIE	► **Falkland (21m-34km)**
FALKLAND	► **Scotlandwell (12m-19km)**
SCOTLANDWELL	► **Kinross (8m-13km)**
KINROSS	► **Abernathy (13m-21km)**
ABERNETHY	► **Cupar (13m-21km)**
CUPAR	► **St Andrews (10m-16km)**

❶ Crail, Fife

Crail's small harbour is a delightful and much photographed place set at the bottom of a steep lane; crab and lobster fishing is carried out from here. Early prosperity stemmed from trading and fishing, and the history of the community is told in the small museum in Marketgate.

⌐i⌐ *Crail Museum and Heritage Centre (seasonal)*

▶ *Continue on the A917 and follow it for 4 miles (6km) to Anstruther.*

❷ Anstruther, Fife

The Scottish Fisheries Museum, which is situated on the seafront, tells the story of fishing and the fisherfolk from this part of the country. In the harbour is moored one of the museum's great attractions, the fishing boat *The Reaper*. One of the houses in the main street is completely decorated with seashells.

⌐i⌐ *East Neuk Information Centre, Scottish Fisheries Museum (seasonal)*

▶ *Continue on the A917 for 1 mile (2km) to Pittenweem.*

❸ Pittenweem, Fife

The busiest fishing port along this coast, there is always lots to see in Pittenweem when the boats are coming in with their catches. Herring used to be the major catch here but now the fishermen concentrate on whitefish.

The religious buildings date back many centuries: the parish church's tower was built in the 16th century and there are remains of a 12th-century priory where witches were 'done to death'.

Nearby St Fillan's Cave is said to be the 7th-century sanctuary of St Fillan. It gave Pittenweem its name (Pittenweem is Pictish for The Place of the Cave).

To the north of

Laid-up fishing boat being painted

Crow-stepped and pantiled houses cluster round Crail harbour, once the haunt of smugglers

Pittenweem stands Kellie Castle, dating from 1360, which has very pleasant sheltered gardens.

▶ *Continue on the A917 for 2 miles (3km) to St Monans.*

❹ St Monans, Fife

St Monans (or St Monance) is a pleasant fishing town, with houses clustered around the local harbour – and its kirk standing almost in the sea.

One rather unusual feature of the town is that it has fewer licensed premises than in neighbouring villages, the result of the town being 'dry' between 1900 and 1947.

To the southwest are the ruins of 17th-century Newark Castle.

▶ *Continue on the A917 for 3 miles (5km) to Elie.*

Fife coastal walk: Elie to St Monans

RECOMMENDED WALKS

The path from St Monans to Elie offers an interesting route past St Monans' church, the ruins of two castles and ends at Elie Ness where there is a fine view of the village. Inland, the walk to the top of East Lomond gives good views over the surrounding countryside.

5 Elie, Fife

This appealing resort offers fine sandy beaches and bathing, golf courses and shelter to the yachts that lie in the harbour. The sea has not always been kind to Elie and the houses along the bay have high walls to protect them. There are many fine 17th-century houses in South Street.

▶ *Continue on the A917 to Upper Largo, then join the A915 to Windygates. Join the A911 and head towards Glenrothes. Turn right at a roundabout at the junction with the A92 and head north-wards. Turn left when the A912 is met and follow this to Falkland.*

6 Falkland, Fife

The village of Falkland is dominated by the very grand palace, which was originally erected by the Stuarts as a royal hunting seat. It dates from the 16th century and stands on a site that has been fortified from the 13th century. The buildings on the southern side of the main court-yard are in a fine state of preservation and have some excellent furnishings; the painted wooden ceilings are particularly good. Within the grounds is a Royal Tennis Court, built in 1539 for James V, before rackets were invented. The game was originally played with the hand, which was protected by a leather glove.

The village itself has numerous fascinating small houses, many of them dating back to the 17th and 18th centuries. The museum in the main street has displays that explain the local history.

▶ *Continue of the A912 and turn left at the A91 and left again at the B919. Turn left at the A911 and follow it to Scotlandwell.*

SPECIAL TO ...

One feature of the houses in many Fife villages are the red pantiles, roofing tiles with a double curve. Although they look costly, they were originally used as they were cheaper than slates. Since they have only small overlaps they often need a lot of mortar between them to keep the roof watertight.

7 Scotlandwell, Tayside

The village is named after the well, a sort of early spa, to which pilgrims travelled during medieval times. Roman soldiers are said to have drunk from it in AD84. However, the present stone cistern dates back only to the 19th century.

▶ *Leave by the B920 and turn right at the B9097. Take another right turn when the B996 is met and follow it to Kinross.*

8 Kinross, Tayside

Kinross, the county town of the former Kinross-shire, stands by the shores of Loch Leven, the largest loch in the Scottish lowlands. Of the loch's two largest islands, St Serf's Island has the remains of a 9th-century priory.

Castle Island is rather nearer the town and can be reached by a local ferry. On it stands Loch Leven Castle, best known as the prison from which Mary, Queen of Scots made her escape in 1568. The castle dates from the 14th century and the building and its garden used to occupy the whole of the island until in the early 19th century the loch's level was lowered, increasing the size of the island. The castle, a five-storey keep, was occupied for about 250 years but was roofless by the end of the 17th century. Kinross town is dominated by imposing Kinross House.

i Kinross Service Area, M90

▶ Continue on the **B996** and join the **A922**. After Milnathort, follow the **B996** then the **A91**. Turn left at the **A912** and right at the **A913** to Abernethy, 13 miles (21 km).

Loch Leven Castle, prison to Mary, Queen of Scots

9 Abernethy, Tayside
One of the main features of this quiet little village is the 11th-century round tower, very similar to Brechin's. Abernethy may have been an important centre in Pictish times and several symbol stones have been found in the vicinity; one of them is set against the wall of the tower.

▶ Continue on the **A913** and follow it for 13 miles (21km) to Cupar.

10 Cupar, Fife
It is rather surprising that this little town, and not St Andrews, was the county town of Fife, but this was due to its central position and because it was the seat of the Thanes (ancient chieftains) of Fife.

Cupar must surely have a place in the history of drama as it was here in 1535 that the first public performance of the satire *Ane satire of the Thrie Estaits* took place. This scorned the church, the nobility and the burgesses of the towns, the three 'estates' that made up the country's ruling bodies. The play has certainly stood the test of time and it is still performed on the Scottish stage.

To the south of Cupar stands the Hill of Tarvit, a mansion house under the ownership of the NTS. The present building was constructed at the beginning of the 20th century to house a fine collection of antique furniture, much of it French. To the west of it is Scotstarvit Tower, a well-preserved five-storey tower house built in the 17th century.

i The Granary, Coal Road (seasonal)

▶ Leave by the **A91** and follow it back to St Andrews.

SCENIC ROUTES

The journey through the fishing villages of East Neuk is very pleasant. Not only are the 'vernacular' houses attractive, there are also views of the coastline, the Isle of May and the opposite shore of the Firth of Forth, with the Bass Rock and Edinburgh obvious landmarks.
Near Loch Leven there are pleasing views of the Lomond Hills which rise steeply from the surrounding rich farmland.

THE NORTHEAST

The Cairngorm mountains, Britain's highest land mass, dominate the northeast of Scotland in many ways. The great glaciers that flowed down from these granite hills during the Ice Age cut their way through the rock, leaving behind a series of river valleys that radiate out from the mountains and flow down to the sea.

In days gone by, it was easier to travel by sea than land and this encouraged coastal settlements to prosper wherever there was a sheltered harbour and the opportunity to trade with other ports, notably those in countries across the North Sea. Today, this coastline boasts some of Britain's most important fishing harbours. But while the fishing industry is long established, it is the North Sea oil developments that have transformed the Aberdeen area and made that city Scotland's 'oil capital'.

The northeast lies in the hills' rain shadow, making this region much drier than the west coast and helping to produce some of Scotland's most profitable farming land. Agriculture continues to be an important industry and much of the region's population lives in scattered towns and villages set among good agricultural land.

The often turbulent times of the Middle Ages saw the establishment of a class of rich farmers, warriors and traders who built keeps, castles and fortified houses. In time, many of these were destroyed while others were extended and embellished and some later transformed into great country houses. Today, we are left with a rich legacy of castles, large and small, reflecting the changing fortunes of family, clan and nation.

The wide variety of landscapes is reflected in the wildlife found in the region. The hills and the high forests are home to deer and birds of prey while the coast, with its sandstone cliffs providing ledges for nesting birds, has countless millions of seabirds.

Walkers, birdwatchers, families seeking tranquil beaches and visitors simply touring around will all find lots to do in this corner of Scotland. To many foreign visitors, Scotland is famous as the home of whisky, and in the northeast a number of internationally famous distilleries are linked together by the 'Malt Whisky Trail', which allows people to learn the secrets of the whisky-making process and inevitably to enjoy a 'wee dram' at the end of a distillery tour.

Traditional Scotsware is sold at MacNaughton's shop at Pitlochry

Farming exhibits from the Falconer Museum, Forres

the small picture-postcard ones like charming Crovie to the big, bustling Peterhead. Each has its own fascination and each reflects the ways in which the sea has been so important to the people of this area. Behind this, the rich countryside, with its landscape of rolling hills, has prosperous farming towns and villages. The long history of settlement in this part of the country is marked by the existence of prehistoric stone circles.

Tour 17

The fact that this tour is the longest one in the region reflects the sheer scale of the Cairngorms. Motorists have to drive round the margins of the

hills, but this does allow the visitor many different opportunities to explore the small glens that cut into the sides of these great mountains. There is much variety on the route; the traditional highland resort of Pitlochry, the more modern Aviemore and the small villages that lie to the east. Walkers will find much to keep them busy on this tour as will followers of other outdoor pursuits.

Tour 18

The visitor to this part of the country might be forgiven for getting the impression there's a castle round every corner! But the district has more to offer than fine old buildings; there are peaceful villages, a rugged coastline and rich agricultural countryside to explore.

A splendid border at Crathes Castle Gardens

Tour 14

Inverness' strategic position at the meeting point of so many land and sea routes has meant that the town and its surrounding district have seen the comings and goings of many different people. Picts, Vikings and warring Scots clans have all left their mark, but the most significant historical event, the battle of Culloden in 1746, has left its mark all over Scotland; in order to understand the history of the Highlands, the battlefields should be visited. This tour encompasses a wide variety of scenery, from the glorious sandy beaches of the Moray Firth to the pine forests that lie below the Cairngorms, which attract tourists throughout the year.

Tour 15

The seaside towns and villages of Moray have much to offer the visitor: picturesque harbours, sandy beaches and a wealth of traditional buildings that give the district its own particular charm. Inland, the districts by the peaty waters of the River Spey are home to many of Scotland's most celebrated whisky distilleries.

Tour 16

The coastal part of this route visits a variety of harbours, from

Land of
Macbeth

1/2 DAYS • 169KM • 106 MILES History and magnificent scenery are ever present on this tour. Just outside Inverness lies Culloden, where the defeat of Bonnie Prince Charlie ruined the last hope of a Stuart restoration to the British throne. Mysteries, too, abound on this tour, from brooding Cawdor Castle, of which Shakespeare's Macbeth was Thane, to the dark waters of Loch Ness which could conceal Britain's most famous monster.

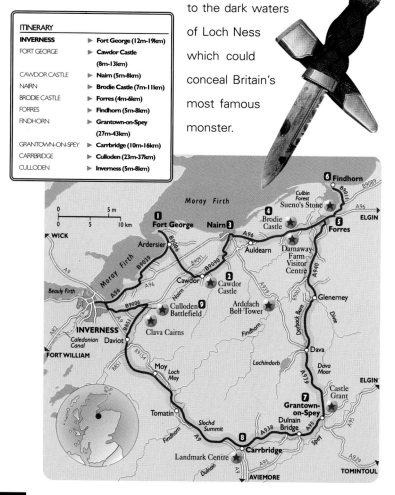

_i_   Castle Wynd

▶ Leave on the **A96**. Turn left at
the **B9039** to reach Ardersier,
then take the **B9006** to Fort
George, a distance of 12
miles (19km).

❶ Fort George, Highland
This outstanding piece of military architecture, which is still
used by the army, was originally
built between 1748 and 1769,
after the Battle of Culloden. It
was guarded by 2000 men and it
has a series of walls, ramparts
and ditches cleverly designed so
that an attacking army would
come under fire from several
positions within the safety of
the fort. It controls the seaward
approach to Inverness as it is
sited on a promontory that juts
into the Moray Firth; this is
rather fortunate for visitors as it
allows good views across the
firth to the Black Isle.

The fort is impressively
huge, indeed the whole of
Edinburgh Castle could fit into
the parade ground! Since the
fort has never seen military
action, very few alterations have
been made to its layout and a
number of original buildings
have been opened to visitors.

The B9006, which leads to
the fort, was one of the military
roads built by Caulfield in the
18th century when the government was trying to 'tame' this
area. It follows the much older
Via Regis (King's Road) which
came from Aberdeen and
crossed the Moray Firth to
Chanonry Point at Fortrose.

▶ Return to Ardersier, then
follow the **B9006** and the
B9090 to Cawdor Castle, 8
miles (13km).

❷ Cawdor Castle, Highland
The castle is dominated by the
great 14th-century tower. Later
additions had far less of a defensive role to play since they were
built in less turbulent times.
Still, the castle has many of the
features that might be expected
of a fortified house such as a
drawbridge, a moat and a prison
that was reached only by a trap
door. The proprietors of Cawdor
were called the Thanes of
Cawdor, a title given by
Shakespeare to Macbeth, but
there is still much speculation
about the real nature of this
warrior king.

To the west stands 15th-century Kilravock Castle, a
massive tower with walls some 7
feet (2m) thick. The tower has
survived through the centuries,
despite the laird backing the
losing side at Culloden, and the
victor, Cumberland, paying it a
visit after the battle. Few castles
in a similar position survived a
visit by the 'Butcher'.

The Woodcock Room at Cawdor
Castle

The golf course at Nairn

▶ Continue on the **B9090** and follow it to Nairn.

3 Nairn, Highland

This popular holiday resort, situated where the River Nairn meets the Moray Firth, has a fine beach, good golf course and activities for family holidays. Charlie Chaplin's favourite holiday resort for many years, it is a prosperous town, with large villas and hotels behind the main centre. Nearer the shore, the former fishermen's houses are tightly packed together in Fishertown where there is a small museum.

To the east, the village of Auldearn was the site of a major battle in 1645 when the Royalist army defeated a force of Covenanters. The battleground can be seen from the top of a 12th-century motte, upon which now sits a 17th-century doocot (dovecot) which has 546 nest holes for pigeons.

i 62 King Street (seasonal)

▶ Leave by the **A96** and turn left at the entrance to Brodie Castle.

FOR HISTORY BUFFS

Highland Ardclach Bell Tower, southeast of Nairn, off the A939, was built in 1655 when the local laird, a Covenanter, was continually being harassed by Royalists. The tower served both as a prison and a watchtower and its bell was used to summon people to the local church.

BACK TO NATURE

Culbin Forest is a large conifer plantation between Nairn and Findhorn, planted in order to stabilise the area of shifting sand. The dunes increased in size during the 17th century and inundated the village of Culbin and its surrounding rich farmland. The forest is now home to varied wildlife, like badgers and capercaillie. Woodland plants include coralroot and twayblade orchids.

4 Brodie Castle, Grampian

Originally, the castle had a Z-plan design, based on a rectangular block with square projecting towers at two opposite corners. This structure, dated 1567, was later added to and has seen many alterations over the centuries. Inside the castle is a good collection of 17th-, 18th- and 19th-century paintings, porcelain and French furniture.

At the eastern entrance to the castle stands the Pictish Rodney's Stone, decorated with a Pictish beast and fish monsters.

▶ Regain the **A96** and continue on it for 4 miles (6km) to Forres.

5 Forres, Grampian

The street pattern in Forres gives clues to the town's antiquity, with a main street wide enough to accommodate a market place and narrow 'wynds' linking the medieval streets. High Street is dominated by the Town House of 1838, built on the site of the old Tolbooth, and the market cross which was erected in 1844. The Falconer Museum in Tolbooth Street has displays of local history, natural history and geology.

The town's main antiquity lies just to the east of Forres, as the B9011 leaves the A96. This is Sueno's Stone, a huge cross-slab monument, over 20 feet (6m) high, carved out of a block of sandstone. It may date back to the 9th century and celebrate a victory by the men of Moray over Vikings based in Orkney.

i *116 High Street (seasonal)*

▶ *Continue on the **A96** then turn left at the **B9011** and follow this to Findhorn.*

6 **Findhorn,** Grampian
This is the third village on this site to be called Findhorn. The first was destroyed by the sea and the second was inundated by shifting sand. The people rebuilt the village near the sea and it was once a prominent port, but its harbour is now given

As well as its many treasures, Brodie Castle also has extensive grounds and a playground

over to pleasure craft. The beaches here are extensive, with huge stretches of sand and dunes along the coast on either side of the River Findhorn's estuary.

▶ *Return along the **B9011** and **A96** to Forres. Head south on the **A940** and join the **A939** for Grantown-on-Spey, 27 miles (43km).*

7 **Grantown-on-Spey,** Highland
This prosperous village, with its sturdy granite buildings along the main street, is a good touring centre for the district. It began as a planned village and from the

start gained a reputation as a place to which Victorian doctors would send patients who were in need of a change of air. Today it is noted for its salmon fishing, and walkers; anglers and families frequent the village during the summer, while in winter it accommodates skiers, Aviemore being only a short drive away.

Standing just to the north of the village, Castle Grant was started in the 15th century but greatly altered in later centuries. Robert Burns visited here during his Highland travels and so did Queen Victoria – though she was not impressed, describing it as a 'very plain looking house, like a factory'.

FOR CHILDREN

To the west of Forres, the Darnaway Farm Visitor Centre gives people the opportunity to see a working dairy farm in action. There is also an exhibition on forestry and a riding centre.

FOR CHILDREN

As well as being endowed with long sandy beaches which will keep children busy for hours on end, Findhorn is a centre for water sports, with sailing, rowing, windsurfing and water skiing available.

[i] *High Street (seasonal)*

▶ *Leave on the **A95** towards Aviemore, and at Dulnain Bridge turn on to the **A938** to Carrbridge*

8 **Carrbridge,** Highland

The old bridge at Carrbridge was built in 1717 after two men drowned at the fording place. The bridge has since lost many of its stones and is precariously balanced over the river making it one of the most photogenic bridges in the country.

The village is a popular touring centre, all the more so because of the nearby Landmark Centre, an entertaining heritage park. It is set in a pine forest and has many walks, including a tree-top trail 20 feet (6m) above the ground.

[i] *Main Street (seasonal)*

▶ *Continue on the **A938** and join the **A9**, heading towards Inverness. Just after Daviot, turn right on the **B851**. Turn left at the **B9006** and follow it to the NTS Visitor Centre at Culloden Moor.*

9 **Culloden,** Highland

Many bloody battles have been fought on Scottish soil, but of all the country's battlefields, Culloden is the saddest. Here, in 1746, the last great battle fought on British soil ended forever the Jacobite hopes of regaining the British crown. It was not a battle of Scots against English, nor was it a battle between different parts of Scotland, but it was the final battle of a long civil war. In its bloody aftermath, the face of the Highlands was changed forever. After the government's victory, the might of the British army was used to subjugate Scotland and to destroy many aspects of the Highlanders' way of life. The battlefield has been laid out to show how the government troops, led by the Duke of Cumberland, faced the army of Charles Edward Stuart (the 'Bonnie Prince Charlie' of song and legend). Displays in the visitor centre describe the course of that dreadful battle, and the equally violent events which followed. Various small memorials on the battlefield indicate where particular clans were buried where they fell, but the principal monument is the Memorial Cairn, erected in 1881. The battle was fought on open moorland and Old Leanach Cottage, which was standing at the time of the battle, still remains. Its reconstructed interior illustrates how Scots people lived at the time of the battle in the mid-18th century.

A little to the east of Culloden, a minor road passes Clava Cairns, some of the most important cairns in the country. The three cairns may have been erected in the Late Stone Age or Early Bronze Age. The two outer ones are called 'passage graves' as a small passageway led through the cairn to a central chamber where bodies or cremated remains were deposited. These cairns have been topped with a massive flat slab and their perimeters were (and still are) marked by a ring of standing stones. Many of these perimeter stones have 'cup marks', small round indentations of unknown origin.

[i] *Daviot Wood, on the A9 (seasonal)*

▶ *Continue along the **B9006** to the **A9**. Join the **A9** and return to Inverness, 5 miles (8km).*

The much-photographed pack-horse bridge at Carrbridge

The Malt Whisky
Trail

1/2 DAYS • 144KM • 89 MILES A tour for all members of the family, taking in as it does the wide, sandy beaches of Moray and the famed Speyside whisky distilleries of Strathisla, Glenfiddich and Glen Grant. The town of Elgin is the starting point for this tour; its many fine buildings, cathedral and ruined castle make it an ideal base which merits further exploration. It's still possible to wander down narrow 'wynds' that link the streets.

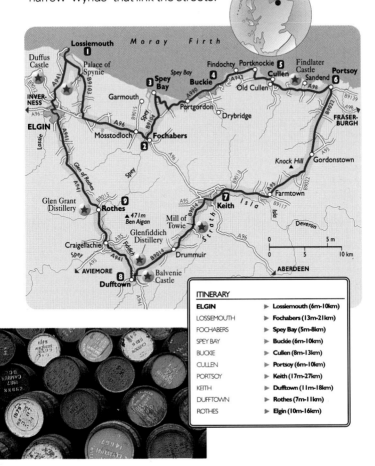

ITINERARY

ELGIN	▶ **Lossiemouth (6m-10km)**
LOSSIEMOUTH	▶ Fochabers (13m-21km)
FOCHABERS	▶ Spey Bay (5m-8km)
SPEY BAY	▶ Buckie (6m-10km)
BUCKIE	▶ Cullen (8m-13km)
CULLEN	▶ Portsoy (6m-10km)
PORTSOY	▶ Keith (17m-27km)
KEITH	▶ Dufftown (11m-18km)
DUFFTOWN	▶ Rothes (7m-11km)
ROTHES	▶ Elgin (10m-16km)

i *17 High Street*

Braco's Banking House in Elgin High Street

FOR HISTORY BUFFS

To the northwest of Elgin stands the ruin of Duffus Castle, on a site that has been fortified from at least the mid-12th century. Originally it was a motte-and-bailey castle but the stone castle now on the motte dates back to the 14th century.

▶ *Leave Elgin on the A941 and follow it north to Lossiemouth.*

❶ Lossiemouth, Grampian
This was developed as a port for landlocked Elgin after its original port of Spynie was cut off from the sea by shifting sand. It later became important during the 19th-century herring boom but today the catches are mainly shellfish and whitefish.

Lossiemouth is now a popular seaside resort, with extensive sandy beaches and a championship golf course. The Lossiemouth Fisheries and Community Museum features many aspects of local life and also has a display dedicated to Ramsay MacDonald, Britain's first Labour Prime Minister, who was born locally.

Just inland stand the ruins of the 15th-century Palace of Spynie, once the seat of the Bishops of Moray.

Duffus Castle is to the southwest of Lossiemouth in an area of flat, fertile farmland, lying only a few feet above sea

FOR CHILDREN

The coast has many good beaches, which makes this area popular with families. Lossiemouth has two beaches; the east one is suitable for surfing while the west one offers safe bathing. Buckie, Elgin and Keith have swimming pools and pony trekking is available at Lossiemouth, Drybridge and Garmouth.

level. This was a swamp when the original motte-and-bailey castle was built. A massive tower was added around 1300. Unfortunately the gravel foundations could not support the extra weight and part of the building's walls gave way and slid downhill.

river's east bank offers good walks and paths leading southward from the village to the very unusual 'earth pillars' which were formed by erosion of the huge quantities of sand and pebble deposits that were laid down here by the Spey.

The factory of Baxters of Speyside is where the well-known tinned soups and other foodstuffs are made and tours round the premises are available. The original Baxter's grocery shop, where the family's soups were first sold in Spey Street, has been reconstructed in the visitor centre and there is also a Victorian kitchen, showing how the family meals were prepared in the 19th century.

The Fochabers Folk Museum in High Street has displays outlining the local history, as well as a costume collection and a display of horse-drawn vehicles.

▶ *Return along the A96, then turn right at the B9104 to Spey Bay, 5 miles (8km).*

3 Spey Bay, Grampian
The River Spey is Scotland's second longest river with a length of 98 miles (158km) and it drains a large area of high ground, including part of the Cairngorms. Huge quantities of ice and water flowed down the river during the Ice Age, accounting for its great width and the massive deposits of sand and gravel brought down at various stages of its history. At Spey Bay, where the river meets the

sea, the river dumps the material it has brought downstream and the huge volume of peaty water stains the sea for quite a distance offshore.

Longshore drift has encouraged a huge shingle spit to form at the river's mouth and salmon fishers have traditionally netted fish from this point. The Tugnet Ice-House, built in 1830 to store the ice that was used for packing salmon, stands near by. This is Scotland's largest ice-house and it has been restored to take on its new role as a museum that tells the story of the salmon fishery.

The bay is the northern terminus for the Speyside Way, the long-distance footpath that follows the river for part of its lower course.

BACK TO NATURE

The coastline is home to many birds who search for food when the tide is out. Spey Bay can be particularly good for birdwatchers with terns, waders, oystercatchers and curlews to be sighted; and keep a look-out for seals a little offshore.

▶ *Return along the B9104 and turn left at an unclassified road to Portgordon. Follow the roads to Portgordon, then join the A990 and follow it to Buckie.*

Household goods on display at the Folk Museum in Fochabers

▶ *Return along the A941 and turn left at the B9103. Turn left at the A96 and continue to Fochabers.*

2 Fochabers, Grampian
Fochabers was originally situated within the grounds of Gordon Castle but was demolished at the end of the 18th century to make way for an extension to the castle. When it was being re-established in its present position, the streets were laid out in a grid pattern, and there still remains a wealth of well-built Georgian houses, especially along its main street. The village's position beside the River Spey led to its growing importance as a river-crossing point, though no bridge crossed the river here until 1804 when the ferry was superseded by Fochabers Old Bridge. The

gamation of smaller fishing communities. Its main harbour is very busy and the area behind it still has many traditional fishermen's houses dating back to the 19th century. The town's rich fishing tradition features strongly in the displays in The Buckie Drifter, the town's Maritime Heritage Centre.

The neighbouring village of Portgordon was once a centre for salmon fishing and near the harbour stands a restored ice-house that was built in 1834.

▶ *Leave by the **A942** via Findochty and Portknockie. Turn left at the **A98** and follow this to Cullen.*

5 Cullen, Grampian
The most obvious feature of this pleasant seaside village is the tall and graceful railway viaduct that slices Cullen in two. Trains no longer run on the line but its route is now part of a coastal path. Below the arches, the seaward part of the village has a little harbour with fishermen's houses and a fine stretch of beach. The golf course is jammed in between the shore and the former sea cliffs and on the course's seaward side stand the Three Kings, three tall sea stacks that have managed to withstand the onslaught of the pounding seas. The Square has many interesting buildings round it, notably the old Town Hall. The very ornate mercat (market) cross was not originally in the Square, but came from Old Cullen which shared the same fate as the original Fochabers, and was demolished because the local laird felt the village was too close to his house. Cullen Auld Kirk, which is still in Old Cullen, dates from

4 Buckie, Grampian
Buckie stretches for about 3 miles (5km) along the coast and has developed through the amal-

Stone buildings above Portsoy harbour, the venue for the annual Scottish Traditional Small Boats Festival

the 16th century and contains some fine stone carvings.

At the western end of Cullen Bay is the curious Bow Fiddle Rock, an island with a natural arch that is probably best seen from the small village of Portknockie, which can be reached via a clifftop path.

To the east of the village stand the ruins of 15th-century Findlater Castle. This was owned by the Ogilvies but abandoned around 1600 in preference to the more comfortable Cullen House.

▶ *Continue on the A98 to Portsoy.*

6 Portsoy, Grampian
Portsoy's sheltered harbour was once considered to be one of the safest in this part of Scotland, an attribute that did much to hasten the port's growth.

The village's great claim to fame, however, was its fine vein of pink and green serpentine stone, in great demand for its

beauty. Some of it was used in the Palace of Versailles. This tradition still lives on and the harbourside Portsoy Marble Workshop has good examples of rock-based ornaments on sale.

▶ *Leave by the A98 and turn right at the B9022. Join the A95 and follow it to Keith.*

7 Keith, Grampian
Keith's role as an important centre for the rich neighbouring farmland reaches its high point each year at the Agricultural Show. Traditional farming ways have been preserved in part at Mill of Towie (to the south of Keith) where oatmeal is produced in a restored 19th-century mill.

The town lies in the broad valley of Strath Isla, hence the name of the local Strathisla Distillery. This is the gateway to the celebrated 'Malt Whisky Trail', a route connecting a number of distilleries that welcome visitors to their premises. Strathisla is the Highlands' oldest working

Cullen harbour, with its famous railway viaduct

Speyside coopers still practising the old craft

[i] *Church Road (seasonal)*

▶ *Leave on the A96 (to Inverness), then turn left at the B9014 which leads into Dufftown.*

[8] **Dufftown,** Grampian

The centre of the village is domi-nated by the battlemented Clock Tower that was built in 1839. The tower has had a varied life, having first been the local gaol, then the burgh (borough) chambers and now a small museum. The clock on the tower came from Banff and played a part in the hanging of the unlucky James MacPherson. This poor fellow was a popular figure who had been robbing the rich and giving the proceeds to the poor, and a petition was raised to obtain a pardon for him. This was successful, but while the pardon was on its way, the local sheriff put the town's clock forward by an hour, making sure that the prisoner was duly dispatched before the reprieve arrived! Dufftown is the home of the Glenfiddich Distillery, which is on the Malt Whisky Trail. Production started here in 1887 and, unusually, the whisky is bottled on the site.

The substantial ruins of Balvenie Castle lie close to the village. This was a massive build-ing surrounding a central court-yard with a curtain wall 7 feet (2m) thick.

distillery: production started in 1786, though illicit brewing and distilling may have taken place on the site as far back as the 13th century. Malt whisky tast-ings are possible, but as there are eight distillerys on the trail it's best to leave the driving to a non-drinker!

[i] *Clock Tower, The Square (seasonal)*

▶ *Leave by the A941 and follow it for 7 miles (11km) to Rothes.*

[9] **Rothes,** Grampian

On the journey from Dufftown to Rothes the A941 crosses the River Spey near the village of Craigellachie. Just upstream from this crossing stands a graceful iron bridge, built by Thomas Telford between 1812 and 1815 to withstand floods when the river was swollen with spring meltwater from the mountains. Its great test came in 1829 when it survived a rise in water level of 15½ feet (4.5m). This is the country's oldest surviving iron bridge.

Founded in 1766 as a croft-ing township (a croft may be best described as a Scottish small holding), Rothes devel-oped into an important centre for distilling as no fewer than five distilleries were working here at one time. The Glen Grant Distillery, which is on the Malt Whisky Trail, was started in 1840 by two brothers and their whisky was one of the first to be bottled as a 'single malt'.

▶ *Continue on the A941 for 10 miles (16km) to return to Elgin.*

SPECIAL TO . . .

The proximity of so many distilleries makes sampling the local whiskies a popular pastime for many visitors. The local tourist information centres can give details. The whisky is matured in oak barrels and at Craigellachie, the Speyside Cooperage produces the barrels using time-honoured skills; there is a visitor centre where you can see the work in progress. The richness of the local fish-ing grounds means that much delicious fresh seafood should be available locally, and in Cullen why not try the local delicacy, 'Cullen Skink', a broth based on smoked haddock?

SCENIC ROUTES

The coastal part of this route is particularly pleasant as there are views of the cliffs, beaches and small settlements with their little harbours. Inland, the route goes through more good arable farming land, though south of Keith sheep farming becomes more important.

The Fishing
Trail

Much of Scotland's wealth has depended on the sea, and this tour takes in the major ports of Fraserburgh and Peterhead as well as the picturesque habours of Crovie and Rosehearty. The tour starts at the town of Banff, whose history as a trading centre has left it with a legacy of fine buildings including the 18th-century Adam-built Duff House.

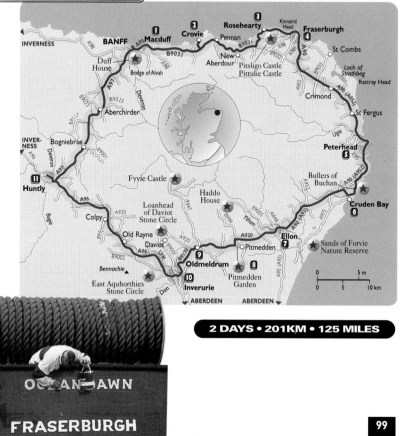

2 DAYS • 201KM • 125 MILES

OCEAN DAWN

FRASERBURGH

ⓘ *Collie Lodge (seasonal)*

RECOMMENDED WALKS

From Duff House, you can walk along a woodland path that leads beside the bank of the River Deveron and across the river's gorge via the Bridge of Alvah. From there, paths and country roads head towards Macduff and back to Banff.

▶ *Leave by the **A98** and follow it for a mile (2km) to Macduff.*

A decaying sea arch looms up from the shore at Tarlair, near Macduff

❶ Macduff, Grampian

This is a busy fishing port and many of the townspeople are connected with some aspect of the industry. There is a week-day fishmarket and boats are still built and repaired in the local boatyard.

Doune Church has a clock tower of which only three of the four sides have faces. The blank face looks towards neighbouring Banff and was deliberately left like that in response to the hanging of James MacPherson when his last-minute reprieve was on its way. The local people felt so enraged at this miscarriage of justice that they wanted to ensure the people of Banff never knew the correct time again.

SCENIC ROUTES

On the journey round the coast, there are spectacular views of the cliffs, beaches and sand dune systems. Perhaps the best sections are between Macduff and Fraserburgh and between Peterhead and Cruden Bay.

▶ *Leave by the **A98** and turn left at the **B9031**. Turn left at the signposted minor road to Crovie.*

❷ Crovie, Grampian

Crovie is one of the gems of the northeast. A tiny village of about 40 houses, most of their gable ends face the shore as some form of protection from the furious sea that laps so close to them. There is no road beside the houses so the villagers use wheelbarrows to carry heavy objects along the sea wall from the car-park to their homes.

BACK TO NATURE

South of the charming little village of Pennan, used as the location for the film *Local Hero*, the Tore of Troup runs inland for about 8 miles (13km). This deep wooded ravine is very sheltered and is home to badgers, mink, foxes and deer; buzzards may also be seen.

▶ *Return to the **B9031** and turn left. Follow this road to Rosehearty, 13 miles (21km).*

❸ Rosehearty, Grampian

Like so many little ports on this coast, Rosehearty's boom time was during the 19th century, when over 130 boats set out to fish for herring from here. Unfortunately, such heady days are long gone and many of the local fishermen work out of Fraserburgh.

Just outside the village lie the ruins of Pitsligo Castle,

Fraserburgh, one of Scotland's
busiest ports

a courtyard castle which
developed from a 15th-century
keep. The building consisted of
only three rooms – a kitchen, a
dining room and a communal
bedroom with 24 beds in it! To
its east is Pittulie Castle, which
dates from the 16th century but
was abandoned in the 19th
century.

FOR CHILDREN

The Northfield Farm Museum,
southwest of New Aberdour,
features an aviary, llamas, farm
machinery and a reconstructed
smiddy.
Good beaches suitable for
family outings are not as
common as in other parts of
this region, but St Combs and
Cruden Bay are well worth
visiting.

▶ *Continue on the **B9031** and
turn left at the **A98** on the
outskirts of Fraserburgh.*

4 Fraserburgh, Grampian
This is one of the busiest
fishing ports in the northeast,
dealing in whiting, cod, sole,
mackerel and herring. The fishmarket is open for business
most days of the week and
there is usually something interesting to watch.

The town is built on the
promontory of Kinnaird Head
(which captured the attention of
the Egyptian geographer
Ptolemy in the 2nd century AD),
and a castle was built here at the
end of the 16th century, later
converted into a lighthouse.
This is now Scotland's
Lighthouse Museum, with
exhibits from around the country. Close to the castle stands
the Wine Tower; this rather odd
building, which has trap doors
instead of an internal staircase,
was erected in the 16th century
but the use to which it was put
is still a mystery. Saltoun
Square, in the centre of the
town, has the old mercat cross
and the Town House,
which was built in 1855.

i Saltoun Square
(seasonal)

▶ *Take the **A90** south
to Peterhead (18
miles/29km)*

5 Peterhead,
Grampian
This was once
Scotland's most impor-
tant whaling centre until
it gave way to the
herring industry in 1818.
Now Europe's busiest
whitefish port and the

SPECIAL TO . . .

This part of Scotland has
important outcrops of granite,
and many towns and villages
on this tour have been built
using this distinctive stone.
Perhaps the most attractive is
Petershead's, which has large
red crystals, quite different
from Aberdeen's medium-
grained blue-grey rock, or the
light grey from Kemnay.
Granite is formed when hot
molten rock, called magma,
cools while still beneath the
earth's surface. The colour of
the resulting rock depends on
the minerals present and the
size of the crystal on how
slowly the rock cools (the
slower the heat loss, the biggar
the crystals).

EU's largest fishing port, there
is also a lot of commercial activity connected with supplying
the North Sea oil rigs. The
Peterhead lifeboat station is
open to visitors. The history of
the whaling and fishing industries is told in the Arbuthnot
Museum and Art Gallery.

▶ *Continue on the **A90**, then
turn left at the **A975** to enter
Cruden Bay.*

6 Cruden Bay, Grampian
This popular summer resort has a long sandy beach and a fine golf course. Visitors may also like to know that the nearby ruins of 17th-century Slains Castle are said to have been the inspiration for the novel *Dracula*. The author, Bram Stoker, used to holiday at Cruden Bay and he began writing his famous gothic tale here in 1895.

A little further up the coast, the sea has carved deep clefts into the tall cliffs, the most spectacular feature being the Bullers of Buchan, a natural arch and a blow hole.

▶ *Leave by the minor road that leads to the **A90**. Turn left at this junction, and follow the **A90** to a right turn at the signposted road to Ellon.*

7 Ellon, Grampian
Ellon was the ancient 'capital' of Buchan, from the time of the Picts up to the defeat of the Norman Comyns who held the land during the Middle Ages. The village gained importance as a crossing point over the River Ythan and its castle had a strategically important role to play in defending the district. Apart from the ruins of the old castle, the other historical remains are the Moot Hill Monument where there was a motte-and-bailey fort to defend the bridge.

Haddo House, to the northwest of the village, is an imposing mansion built by William

Caption: Shiny copper drums at the Glengarrioch Distillery

Adam in 1732, though much of the interior was redecorated around 1880. The house, which is owned by the NTS, has extensive parklands with walks and an adventure playground.

i   *Market Street Car Park (seasonal)*

▶ *Leave by the **A920** and follow it to Pitmedden House (a little to the northwest of Pitmedden).*

8 Pitmedden Garden, Grampian
The gardens at Pitmedden were laid out in the 17th century and the formal garden is made up of elaborate geometric designs filled with brilliantly coloured flowers. The Museum of Farming Life, in the grounds of the estate, has many exhibits of tools and farm machinery from the past. The graveyard in

Udny Green, just south of Pitmedden, contains a rather bizarre little building – a circular mort house, built in 1832 to thwart body snatchers. Coffins were placed in here on a turntable, then removed for burial after a maximum stay of three months, the idea being that they would be quite unsuitable for digging up and sale by then.

▶ *Continue on the **A920** and join the **A947** to Oldmeldrum.*

9 Oldmeldrum, Grampian
The village retains its medieval street pattern, with the large Town Hall dominating the market square. Tucked away on the outskirts of the village is the Glengarrioch Distillery, on a site said to have had a distillery in 1797. The distilling process consumes a great deal of energy and one rather novel feature of this distillery is that its waste heat is used to grow tomatoes in glasshouses.

BACK TO NATURE

The Sands of Forvie National Nature Reserve is a vast dune system that has in the past overwhelmed settlements. It is also home to many birds including arctic terns, Sandwich terns, eider ducks and shelducks. Sea ducks are particularly numerous in the winter, along with divers and grebes.

To the west of the village lies the little settlement of Daviot, just beyond which is the celebrated Loanhead of Daviot stone circle. This imposing circle was constructed about 5000 years ago and perhaps used in viewing the passage of the moon or in various local rites and customs. The most important part of the circle was the huge recumbent boulder which was put into position so that its uppermost face was horizontal. Ten upright boulders were then placed in a circle to complete the structure. The circle was later used for burials and cremations.

Carved entrance to Huntly Castle

FOR HISTORY BUFFS

Fyvie Castle, northwest of Oldmeldrum, has undergone many changes from its original 13th-century structure but is known as the 'crowning glory of Scots baronial architecture'. The finest feature is the 13-foot (4m) wide stone staircase.

▶ *Leave on the **A920** and bear left at the **B9170** to Inverurie.*

10 Inverurie, Grampian

This busy little town is the main shopping and administrative centre for the surrounding district. Its wide main street is dominated by the Town Hall, built in Grecian style in 1863.

The town's position at the confluence of the Don and the Urie has given it some importance for a long time and a medieval motte called The Bass stands by the River Urie. West of the town, minor roads lead to Easter Aquhorthies stone circle which has a massive recumbent stone and a circle of smaller uprights.

i *Town Hall, Market Place (seasonal)*

▶ *Leave by the **A96** to Huntly.*

The Brandsbutt Stone near Inverurie, which bears ancient Pictish symbols

11 Huntly, Grampian

The long straight main road of this neat little town passes under the arch of the Gordon Schoos and heads towards the impressive ruins of Huntly Castle, one of the finest castles in this part of the country. A 12th-century Norman motte is still to be seen. Construction of the palace was started beside it in the mid-15th century. The most important decorative features are the carved entrance doorway and the fireplaces. Remarkably, for a roofless building of this age, some of the plasterwork still survives –

complete with original graffiti! The castle also had its own prison, a dreadful place formed out of a pit cut deep into the foundations.

i *7a The Square (seasonal)*

▶ *Return eastwards to and continue along the **A96**, then turn left after a short distance at the **A97** to return to Banff.*

Around the
Cairngorms

Rugged granite mountains and forested glens are the major features of this tour through the Cairngorms. Pitlochry, one of the Highland's most attractive tourist resorts, nestles below the hills on the eastern bank of the River Tummel and makes a very pleasant Highland base.

2/3 DAYS • 327KM • 204 MILES

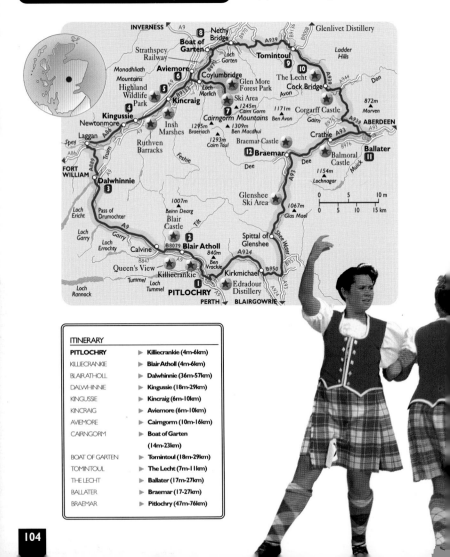

ITINERARY

PITLOCHRY	▶ **Killiecrankie (4m-6km)**
KILLIECRANKIE	▶ **Blair Atholl (4m-6km)**
BLAIR ATHOLL	▶ **Dalwhinnie (36m-57km)**
DALWHINNIE	▶ **Kingussie (18m-29km)**
KINGUSSIE	▶ **Kincraig (6m-10km)**
KINCRAIG	▶ **Aviemore (6m-10km)**
AVIEMORE	▶ **Cairngorm (10m-16km)**
CAIRNGORM	▶ **Boat of Garten**
	(14m-23km)
BOAT OF GARTEN	▶ **Tomintoul (18m-29km)**
TOMINTOUL	▶ **The Lecht (7m-11km)**
THE LECHT	▶ **Ballater (17m-27km)**
BALLATER	▶ **Braemar (17-27km)**
BRAEMAR	▶ **Pitlochry (47m-76km)**

SCENIC ROUTES

The whole of this route offers
memorable scenery, but
perhaps the most attractive
parts are near Blair Atholl, the
views of Cairn Gorm and the
journey from Donside to
Deeside. One very well-known
viewpoint just off the route is
the Queen's View, which is at
the eastern end of Loch
Tummel.

► Leave on the **B8079**, then
turn right at the A9 and head
towards Inverness. Bear left
at the **A889** and follow to
Dalwhinnie.

8 Dalwhinnie, Highland
At an altitude of 1,188 feet
(362m), this is the highest
village in the Highlands and
was an important stopping place
in the days when the main high-
way passed through here. It has
a small distillery which is open
to the public.

► Continue on the **A889** and
turn right at the **A86** to
Kingussie.

Britain's only private army on
display at Blair Atholl

[i] 22 Atholl Road

► Leave Pitlochry by the **A924**,
then the **B8019** for about
1 1/2 miles (2km) before turning on to the **B8079** to the
National Trust for Scotland
Visitor Centre at Killiecrankie.

1 Killiecrankie, Tayside
The wooded gorge of
Killiecrankie is a strategic pass
through the Highlands. A deci-
sive battle was fought near here
in 1689 when a Jacobite army
defeated a government force. In
the aftermath of the battle, one
of the Government soldiers,
Donald MacBean, escaped from
his pursuers by jumping 18 feet
(6m) across the River Garry at a
point now known as the
'Soldier's Leap'.

FOR HISTORY BUFFS

The two ends of Glen Tilt are
met during this tour – at Blair
Atholl and at Braemar. This was
an historically important route
across the Highlands but is
now the preserve of walkers.
In 1861 Queen Victoria passed
through it in her carriage,
travelling 69 miles (111km) in
one day! Earlier, in the 1840s,
the Duke of Atholl attempted
to close this right of way; the
story is celebrated in The
Ballad of Glen Tilt.

Hammer-throwing at the Pitlochry
Highland Games

[i] NTS Visitor Centre (seasonal)

► Continue on the **B8079** for 4
miles (6km) to Blair Atholl.

2 Blair Atholl, Tayside
This little village, situated
where the Tilt and Garry rivers
meet, is dominated by Blair
Castle, home of the Dukes of
Atholl. The oldest part of the
castle, Comyn's Tower, dates
back to 1269 but much of the
present structure is relatively
'modern'. At the end of the 18th
century the castle
was completely
renov-ated; parapets
and towers were
removed and it was
turned into a
Georgian mansion.
The picturesque
towers and crow-
stepped gables
were later additions
when the Scots
baronial style came
into fashion. The
castle has extensive
grounds with many
fine walks. The
Duke of Atholl is
the only man in
Britain to have a
private army, a
right granted him
by Queen
Victoria.

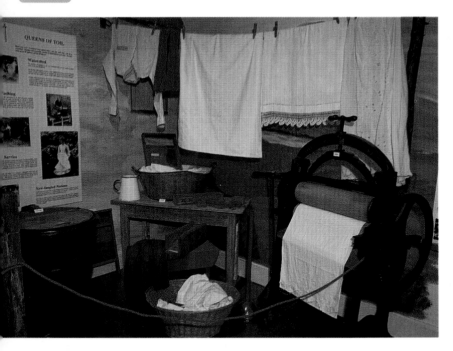

4 Kingussie, Highland

The main attraction here is the Highland Folk Museum and the most fascinating exhibit is the 'black house', built in the manner of the drystone houses that were common on the island of Lewis. Other exhibits focus on Highland agriculture, the life of the tinkers (travelling people) and the furniture used in Highland houses over the last 300 years.

Across the River Spey stands the gaunt ruins of Ruthven Barracks which were built in 1719 but destroyed by the Jacobite army in 1746 to prevent their use by the Hanoverians.

i King Street; Ralia, on the A9 near Newtonmore (both seasonal)

▶ *Leave by the B9152 and follow it for 6 miles (10km) to Kincraig.*

Highland cattle at Kincraig Highland Wildlife Park

Highland Folk Museum: Washing day exhibit

5 Kincraig, Highland

The Highland Wildlife Park at Kincraig is home for a collection of animals that once roamed here freely. Reindeer, wild horses, brown bears, wolves, lynx and even bison were at one time native to this part of Scotland. Now they can only be seen from the safety of a car when driving through the park.

The village stands by Loch Insh, which has a water sports centre, while further up the Spey the river widens at Insh

SPECIAL TO . . .

There are numerous whisky distilleries in the area which offer guided tours round the premises and the chance to sample their particular malt. Shinty (which is similar to hockey) is very popular in the Kingussie/Newtonmore area and an opportunity to see a game should not be missed. For presents, have a look at jewellery incorporating 'cairngorms', the smoky semi-precious stones that are found in the area.

Marshes. This is Scotland's largest inland marsh with a reserve administered by the RSPB (Royal Society for the Protection of Birds). It is particularly good for waders and wildfowl.

Strathspey Railway locomotive at Boat of Garten

FOR CHILDREN

The wildlife park at Kincraig and the reindeer herd at Cairngorm are worth seeing. There are lots of outdoor activities, both land and water-based, available in the area near Aviemore and the indoor facilties in the town offer useful wet-weather alternatives.

▶ *Continue on the **B9152** for 6 miles (10km) to Aviemore.*

6 **Aviemore,** Highland
Until the 1960s Aviemore was just another small Highland village, but the huge leisure complex that was then established has transformed it into the busiest tourist centre in the Highlands. The new buildings sit uneasily in the Highland landscape, but they offer many

The Cairngorms: view to Loch Morlich and Aviemore

indoor facilities that are not found elsewhere in the area, hence its popularity, especially with winter visitors who come flocking here to ski in the Cairngorms.

Aviemore has a station on the Perth to Inverness railway line and it is also at the southern end of the Strathspey Railway; run by enthusiasts, it is based in Boat of Garten.

⌊i⌋ *Grampian Road*

▶ *Take the Cairngorm road out of Aviemore. Follow it through Coylumbridge, past Loch Morlich and up the mountain road to the Coire Cas ski slopes at Cairngorm.*

7 **Cairngorm,** Highland
The Cairngorm mountains are formed from a massive dissected plateau of granite with an altitude of around 4,000 feet (1,220m). The chairlift at Coire Cas is operated through-out the year and climbs to a restaurant near the summit of Cairn Gorm, but it should be remembered that even though it is calm and sunny at the chair-lift car-park, it can be very windy and bitterly cold near the summit. The Cairngorm plateau is covered with frost-shattered boulders which give little shelter to man or beast,

but it does support a herd of reindeer which were introduced here in 1952.

The Rothiemurchus estate and the Glen More Forest Park lie between Aviemore and the Cairngorms and there are many attractive low-level walks through the stands of Scots pine and around Loch Morlich, which is a popular water-sports centre.

▶ *Return to Coylumbridge and turn right at the B970. Follow this towards Boat of Garten and turn left at a signposted unclassified road close to the village.*

8 Boat of Garten, Highland

The name derives from a chain-operated ferry across the Spey that was replaced in 1899 by a substantial bridge. This is the home of the Strathspey Railway, one of the finest tourist attractions in the area, particularly for those nostalgic for the days of steam! With some of the best views of any preserved steam railroad in Britain, the Strathspey Railway line runs along a scenic route to Aviemore.

East of the village stands Abernethy Forest, part of the old Caledonian Forest, where there are many splendid Scots pines. Beside Loch Garten, which lies within the forest, is an osprey breeding site and many birdwatchers come here each year to witness the progress of the current pair. The ospreys were hunted out of the Highlands altogether at the end of the 19th century, but in the 1950s one nest was discovered in the district. Nowadays, the RSPB maintains a close guard on the nest and visitors can watch the birds from a covered hide. People who spend some time in the district may be fortunate enough to see an osprey fishing in one of the lochs.

BACK TO NATURE

The ospreys at Loch Garten RSPB reserve are the most obvious example of how wild animals are being encouraged to re-populate their old haunts. This is assisted by the careful management of the remains of the old Caledonian Forest in the area to the north of Cairngorm. Visitors should also look for Scottish crossbills and crested tits in the pine forest, and golden-eye ducks and Slavonian grebes on the lochs.

Early morning mist rising above Loch Morlich

▶ *Return along the unclassified road to the B970 and then turn left, and follow this road to Nethy Bridge. Turn right after crossing the River Nethy and follow an unclassified road to the A939. Turn right at this junction to reach Tomintoul.*

9 Tomintoul, Grampian

This is another of the Highlands' highest villages and its position means that its weather can be rather unpredictable, with snow not unknown in June!

It has a broad main street and a large central square with the local museum. Although there are only a few shops, one which will be of interest to many visitors is the well-stocked Whisky Castle, which has a vast array of whiskies from many parts of Scotland.

To the north stands the Glenlivet Distillery, which is famous throughout the whisky-drinking world; it has a visitor centre and offers tours.

ℹ *The Square (seasonal)*

▶ *Continue on the A939 to the skiing area at The Lecht.*

10 The Lecht, Grampian
Just beyond the Lecht stands the imposing Corgarff Castle. The loop-holed curtain wall surrounding it was added after the 1745 uprising in order that the Government might use the castle to police this strong Jacobite centre.

Winter visitors should take care if snow is forecast as the Tomintoul to Cock Bridge section of the A939 is sometimes blocked by winter snow.

▶ *Continue on the **A939** then turn left at the **A93** for Ballater.*

11 Ballater, Grampian
Deeside became fashionable after Queen Victoria built a summer retreat at nearby Balmoral Castle. The popularity of 'Royal Deeside' was further increased when the railway line, now closed, was built but it only ventured as far as Ballater as the Queen did not wish her peace and quiet to be disturbed! A small exhibition about the local railway line is housed in the tourist information centre. The town is a good centre from which to explore Deeside, and its solidly built granite houses make it a pleasant place to stroll around. The present Balmoral Castle was built in 1855 with local granite and is a fine example of the Scots baronial style. It is the Scottish home of the British royal family and the grounds are open to the public during part of the summer.

☐ *Station Square (seasonal)*

▶ *Return along the **A93** and continue to Braemar.*

12 Braemar, Grampian
The village is situated in an important position at the junction of three glens and there have been fortifications here from at least 1390 when Kindrochit Castle (now a ruin) was built in what is now the centre of the village. Outside the village, Braemar Castle is a good example of a Hanoverian

fort which was used to police the Highlands. Built in 1628, it is open to the public.

The Jacobite uprising of 1715 began here and the Invercauld Arms Hotel stands on the site where the standard was raised at the start of the campaign to put a Stuart back on the British throne.

Braemar can be busy at times, but never more so than in September when crowds flock to the local Highland games, the Braemar Gathering. The royal family are regular visitors and among the most popular events are the bagpipe playing competitions and the tossing of the caber. Sport is not new to the village, and in the 11th century King Malcolm Canmore, who needed a messenger, held a race here to find the fastest man.

☐ *The Mews, Mar Road*

RECOMMENDED WALKS

There are popular walks of all standards throughout this tour and most tourist information centres have small booklets outlining good walks in their localities. Interesting starting points include Pitlochry, Killiecrankie, the Rothiemurchus and Glen More area, and the upper reaches of the Dee beyond Braemar.

▶ *Continue on the **A93** past the Glenshee skiing area at Cairnwell and turn right at the **B950**. Turn right again when the road meets the **A924** and follow this road back to Pitlochry.*

Balmoral Castle, reputedly the Queen's favourite residence

The Castle
Trail

Aberdeen, the 'Granite City', is the gateway to Royal Deeside and to the great spread of historic houses known as the Castles of Mar. Aberdeen itself is a fascinating city which has gained a reputation for its flowers, while Old Aberdeen has many buildings dating back to medieval times.

2 DAYS • 230KM • 143 MILES

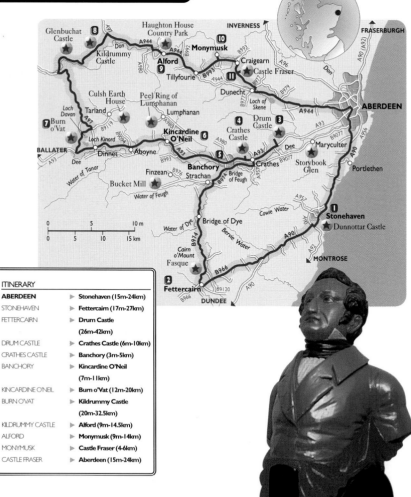

ITINERARY		
ABERDEEN	▶	Stonehaven (15m-24km)
STONEHAVEN	▶	Fettercairn (17m-27km)
FETTERCAIRN	▶	**Drum Castle**
		(26m-42km)
DRUM CASTLE	▶	**Crathes Castle (6m-10km)**
CRATHES CASTLE	▶	**Banchory (3m-5km)**
BANCHORY	▶	**Kincardine O'Neil**
		(7m-11km)
KINCARDINE O'NEIL	▶	**Burn o'Vat (12m-20km)**
BURN O'VAT	▶	**Kildrummy Castle**
		(20m-32.5km)
KILDRUMMY CASTLE	▶	**Alford (9m-14.5km)**
ALFORD	▶	**Monymusk (9m-14km)**
MONYMUSK	▶	**Castle Fraser (4-6km)**
CASTLE FRASER	▶	**Aberdeen (15m-24km)**

i St Nicholas House, Broad Street

SPECIAL TO . . .

When in Aberdeen, look out for Aberdeen butteries in the baker's shops. These are made from a butter-rich dough and are similar to French croissants.

▶ Leave by the **A90** and turn left at the minor road that leads to Stonehaven, 15 miles (24km).

Exhibit at the Aberdeen Maritime Museum

i Allardice Street (seasonal)

❶ Stonehaven, Grampian
As well as being a port with a long-established harbour, Stonehaven also has the beaches and other facilities that attract many visitors. The oldest part of the town has a 16th-century Tolbooth which is now used as a museum with special emphasis on local history and the fishing industry. Above the town, the war memorial stands on a hilltop which offers fine views of the coast and the countryside.

The Scots are well renowned for their celebrations at Hogmanay and Stonehaven celebrates the close of the old year with its Fireball Festival. The 'ceremony' may stem from ancient pagan rites, and as the Town House bells strike midnight, the participants march up High Street twirling burning balls of rags and twigs round their heads.

To the south of the town is Dunnottar Castle, a 14th-century building on a site fortified since the 5th century. The castle stands on a dramatically positioned headland and in 1651 to 1652 it was able to withstand eight months of siege by Cromwell's army before having to surrender. It was also the place where Scotland's royal regalia was hidden from Cromwell.

Dramatic Dunnottar Castle overlooking the sea

BACK TO NATURE

At Fowlsheugh, about 3 miles (5km) to the south of Stonehaven, the RSPB manages the largest seabird colony on the British mainland, with no fewer than 80,000 breeding pairs of birds raising their young on the steep cliffs that plunge into the sea. Guillemots, razorbills, kittiwakes and fulmars are among the birds to be seen here.

▶ Take the **A90** south. After 7
miles (11km) turn right at
the **B966** to Fettercairn.

Fettercairn, Grampian

The older houses in this little
village are built from a red-
coloured sandstone, much
warmer-looking than the rather
austere grey of the granites so
common around the Aberdeen
area. The mercat cross stands in
the village square and dates
back to 1670. In comparison to
this traditional piece of local
architecture, a large and very
ostentatious Gothic arch celebrates a visit by Queen Victoria
in 1861.

Fettercairn Distillery stands
on the village outskirts and
tours round it are available. The
original building was established in 1820. To the north
stands the estate of Fasque,
which is open to the public.
This was the home of William
Gladstone, four times Prime
Minister. Many of the rooms
have changed little since the
house was built in the 1820s and
there is a wealth of Victorian
artefacts, especially in the
kitchens.

▶ Leave by the **B974** on the
Cairn o' Mount road and
head towards Banchory. Just
before the town, turn right at
a minor road (to Kirkton of
Durris) and follow this along
the southern bank of the

Fasque House in Fettercairn; one-
time home to Prime Minister
William Gladstone

River Dee. Turn left at the
A957 to reach Crathes. Turn
right at the **A93** and then left
at an unclassified road to
Drum Castle.

Drum Castle, Grampian

The old Tower of Drum was
built in the 13th century with
walls 12 feet (4m) thick. Beside
it the relatively 'modern' 17th-
century house has particularly
interesting domestic rooms. The
buildings stand in the Old Wood
of Drum, a remnant of the

ancient Caledonian Forest, and many large oaks, pines and wild cherry trees still flourish here, while a walled garden houses a collection of historic roses spanning four centuries.

The splendid gardens surrounding Crathes Castle

▶ *Return to the **A93** and turn right. Turn right at the entrance to Crathes Castle.*

4 Crathes Castle,
Grampian
This L-shaped tower house was built in the 16th century and contains notable interior decoration. The painted ceilings are exceptionally fine – these date from the late 16th century and very early 17th century and feature ancient and mythical heroes such as Hector, Alexander the Great and King Arthur. The gardens, which are set within yew hedges that are about 300 years old, contain some excellent examples of the art of topiary.

▶ *Continue on the **A93** for 3 miles (5km) to Banchory.*

The vibrantly painted ceiling at Crathes Castle

5 Banchory, Grampian
Situated at the confluence of the River Dee and the Water of Feugh, Banchory is a pleasant little Highland town which is a good base from which to explore the area. There is a local history museum in Bridge Street. Close to the village, the Bridge of Feugh spans a little gorge and this has become a very popular place to watch salmon leaping their way upstream.

This is good farming country and numerous old farm buildings survive. One of these, to the southwest of Banchory, is the restored 19th-century wood-turning mill at Finzean. This remained in use until 1974, and was then abandoned, but the mill is now happily refurbished to continue turning wooden buckets, hence its more usual name, the Bucket Mill.

i Bridge Street

▶ *Continue on the **A93** for 7 miles (11km) to Kincardine O'Neil.*

6 Kincardine O'Neil,
Grampian
This small village gained early importance for its position at the Deeside side of the Cairn O' Mount route, and a ferry

crossed the river here, later superseded by a bridge in the 13th century. This is one of Deeside's oldest villages and it has a very fine ruined church, built in 1233 and associated with a hospice for travellers.

FOR HISTORY BUFFS

To the north of Kincardine O'Neil lies the village of Lumphanan, where Macbeth is said to have been killed, and to its southwest stands the Peel Ring of Lumphanan, one of the region's earliest earthworks. It dates from the 13th century and the buildings that were stationed on the mound were protected by a wide ditch.

▶ *Continue on the A93 and turn right at the B9119. Turn left at the car-park for the Burn o'Vat.*

7 Burn o' Vat, Grampian
The area around the Vat has been laid out with paths to guide visitors round the many examples showing how the landscape was formed during the Ice Age, about 12,000 to 15,000 years ago. Huge rivers and streams carried vast quantities of rock debris down from the ice-covered mountains and as they did so carved out gullies and gorges and dumped the debris on the low-lying land to the east. The Burn o' Vat itself is a huge bottle-shaped pot-hole that was worn out of the solid rock by the rushing water. It is some 65 feet (20m) in diameter, and its base is filled with sand and gravel.

Lochs Davan and Kinord lie to the east. These are 'kettle holes', formed where huge stranded blocks of ice eventually melted. There are a number of pleasant walks round Loch Kinord and on the northern shore of the loch is the Kinord cross-slab, a 9th-century granite Celtic cross.

The district known as Cromar, which lies to the north and east of the Vat has numerous monuments that indicate its occupation by ancient peoples over a long time. One unusual structure is the Culsh Earth House which was found at Culsh Farm, on the B9119, after Tarland. This was probably a storehouse built over 2,000 years ago.

▶ *Continue on the B9119 heading northeast. Turn left at the A97 in order to reach Kildrummy Castle.*

8 Kildrummy Castle, Grampian
Before reaching Kildrummy, Glenbuchat Castle is passed at a bend in the River Don. This 16th-century castle was built above the ravine of

The 18th century Bridge of Feugh spanning the River Feugh, from which visitors can watch salmon leap

Artefact found during excavations at Kildrummy Castle

the Water of Buchan by John Gordon, and above the door of the southwest tower he had carved the rather philosophical inscription 'nothing on arth remains bot faime'.

The great medieval castle of Kildrummy lies on raised ground near the River Don. This was once one of the north's most important castles and, although now in ruins, many of its surrounding walls still stand. It survived numerous sieges but in 1306, when Robert the Bruce's brother was defending it against English attack, he was betrayed by a smith named Osbarn. Legend has it the gold he was promised for his treachery was poured down his throat, molten!

▶ *Continue on the **A97**, then turn right on to the **A944** which leads to Alford.*

9 **Alford,** Grampian
This is the home of the Grampian Transport Museum where visitors can enjoy such diverse exhibits as horse-drawn vehicles, vintage cars, a road roller and even a huge snow plough. One very unusual vehicle is the steam-driven car called the 'Craigievar Express', built by the local postman at

Exhibit from the Grampian Transport Museum, Alford

Craigievar in 1895. It has three wheels and he used it to carry the post on his round.

The village was the terminus of a railway line from Aberdeen and the former station of the Great Northern Scottish Railway now houses a museum. A narrow-gauge railway runs to Haughton House Country Park and Murray Park. Alford's former cattle market has been preserved and now houses a rural life museum.

i *Railway Museum, Station Yard (seasonal)*

▶ *Continue on the **A944** and turn left at the **B993**. Turn left at a minor road to enter Monymusk, 9 miles (14km).*

10 **Monymusk,** Grampian
This quiet little village, sited just off the main road, has a splendid Norman church dating back to the 12th century, when an Augustinian priory was also built. The village is laid out very neatly in the fashion of a planned 'estate village', with a little grassy area in its centre. A former toll house stands at the junction of the B993 and the road into the village.

▶ *Return to the **B993** and turn left. Turn right at a minor road to Craigearn, then right again to Castle Fraser.*

11 **Castle Fraser,** Grampian
The castle, topped with the usual turrets and towers of the Scots baronial style, originated as a rectangular tower in the mid-15th century. Later additions and alterations transformed it into a handsome mansion house. The Round Tower gives an excellent view of the rest of the building and in particular all the different designs of small towers that decorate the upper part of the building. The estate gardens are very pleasant and well worth visiting.

▶ *Turn left after leaving the castle grounds and follow the unclassified road to the **B977** where a right turn is taken. Turn left at the **A944** to return to Aberdeen.*

RECOMMENDED WALKS

There are many popular walks in this area and most tourist information centres have leaflets with information on them, including forest walks, in their area. Places of particular interest include Burn o'Vat, Haughton House Country Park and the West Gordon Way (which passes near Alford).

THE HIGHLANDS & ISLANDS

Nowhere else in Britain can match the Scottish Highlands and Islands for sheer splendour. The grand mountains, heather-clad hillsides and indented coastline (complete with some of Britain's best beaches) make this classic touring country.

The west coast, with its long broken coastline, provides the most dramatic scenery. Communities are few and far apart in some districts, leaving the land to the sheep, the cattle and the midges. The east coast and the Great Glen are more populated and offer better facilities.

This historic region abounds with tales and legends of saints and Picts, of Viking invaders and endlessly warring native clans. It is a long history, much of it bloodied with battles, and it has left the countryside rich in antiquities, and burial chambers, standing stones, brochs, forts and castles which can be seen wherever people found land to settle. However, in the last 200 years, the proportion of Scots living in the Highlands and Islands has more than halved. Many people have been forced off the land, as during the infamous Highland Clearances which spanned the mid-18th to the late 19th centuries, when landowners chose to evict their tenants, destroy their homes, and turn the land over to more profitably exploit-able tenants – sheep. Many joined the population drift to the Central Belt of Scotland where work was to be found. But many Highland communities are now finding that their population is rising again, as more 'incomers' discover the high quality of life.

The view towards the Isles of Rum and Eigg from Arisaig

Visitors will find that certain events in Scottish history crop up again and again as they tour round the region. The Highland Clearances, the feuding between the clans, the Jacobite Uprising of 1745, the boom and slump of the herring industry: these and many other landmarks in Scotland's history shaped the country and have been well recorded in many monuments, large and small.

Above all, it is the people that make up the country and those that live and work in the Highlands and Islands are having to adapt to great changes. Many rely on the land for a living, but new skills are being learned, new trades taken up and new visitors welcomed to the delights of this part of Scotland.

Tour 19

West of the Highland 'gateway' of Fort William, great fingers of land stick out into the sea. These peninsulas have scattered crofting communities that are linked by narrow twisting roads offering new views round every corner. Road conditions dictate that progress will not be fast, but then that is no drawback when travelling through one of the least visited parts of the mainland, where each bay and glen is worthy of exploration.

Tour 20

The length of this tour reflects the paucity of major cross-country routes in the Highlands and the extent to which the sea lochs bite into the west coast. This is the Highlands at its best, with giant mountains providing the backdrop to some unforgettable beaches. Inland, the Great Glen carves a wide gash in the fabric of the land and this cross-country route had been followed over the millennia by settlers, hunters, missionaries, soldiers – and even sailors!

Tour 21

Two cross-country routes link the eastern village of Bonar Bridge with more dramatic west coast scenery. Europe has few wildernesses left, but as visitors approach the uninhabited moor and mountain area of Inverpolly, they can get some feeling of just how starkly beautiful (and inhospitable!) the Highland

Passenger boat leaving Iona for Staffa

landscape can be. However, the rich harvest from the sea provides many communities with a good livelihood and helps maintain the Highland crofting traditions.

Tour 22

Much of this long tour around the top of Scotland follows the narrow populated coastal fringe. There seems to be almost no limit to the number of beautiful sandy beaches to be found here, and many of them will be deserted. Caithness, set in a much gentler landscape than Sutherland, has something of a timeless quality about it, especially in the farming areas, and it is rich in prehistoric antiquities that continue to puzzle archaeologists to this day.

Tour 23

In many ways, Easter Ross and the Black Isle are very different from the rest of the region. This is particularly good farming country, with large prosperous farms and bustling towns. The blend of gentler Highland landscape with the facilities of seaside resorts makes this district popular with families and those seeking a relaxed tour through pleasant countryside.

Tour 24

Skye, the 'Misty Isle', draws visitors to its shores eager to see the rugged grandeur of the Cuillin Hills and to experience a place where time passes more slowly than on the mainland. The island is so steeped in tradition and history, and has such splendid scenery that it lures visitors back time and again.

Tour 25

With its interior composed largely of mountain, moorland and bog, Mull's coastline roads link villages, harbours, farms and castles. The sea is never far away, and with a coastline some 300 miles (480km) long the views towards the sea are as fine as they are varied.

Kittiwakes on Handa's cliffs

The Road To
The Isles

Fort William is often referred to as the Gateway to the Highlands, and although not essentially a tourist resort, it does have a wealth of services and shops for books, tartans, tweeds and outdoor wear. Just outside the town lies Ben Nevis, at 4,406 feet (1,344m), Britain's highest mountain.

2/3 DAYS • 315KM • 195 MILES

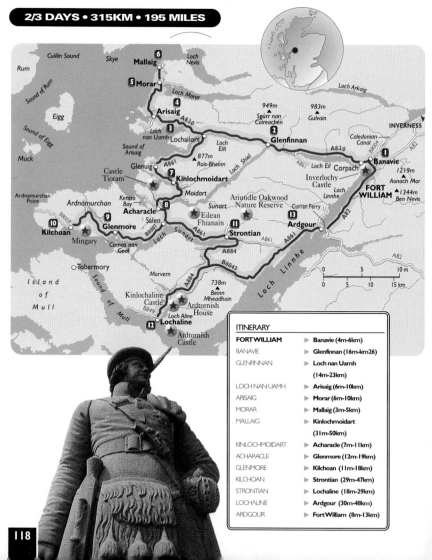

ITINERARY

FORT WILLIAM	▷	**Banavie (4m-6km)**
BANAVIE	▷	**Glenfinnan (16m-km26)**
GLENFINNAN	▷	**Loch nan Uamh (14m-23km)**
LOCH NAN UAMH	▷	**Arisaig (6m-10km)**
ARISAIG	▷	**Morar (6m-10km)**
MORAR	▷	**Mallaig (3m-5km)**
MALLAIG	▷	**Kinlochmoidart (31m-50km)**
KINLOCHMOIDART	▷	**Acharacle (7m-11km)**
ACHARACLE	▷	**Glenmore (12m-19km)**
GLENMORE	▷	**Kilchoan (11m-18km)**
KILCHOAN	▷	**Strontian (29m-47km)**
STRONTIAN	▷	**Lochaline (18m-29km)**
LOCHALINE	▷	**Ardgour (30m-48km)**
ARDGOUR	▷	**Fort William (8m-13km)**

The Road To The Isles

☑ *Cameron Square*

'Neptune's Staircase': a series of eight locks on the Caladonian Canal

SPECIAL TO . . .

The Ben Nevis Hill Race, which takes place on the first Saturday in September each year, attracts competitors from far and wide. Starting from close to sea level, this gruelling race to the summit and back is only for the fittest of athletes. The record time is 1 hour, 25 minutes and 34 seconds.

▶ *Leave by the **A82** (to Inverness), then turn left at the **A830** (to Mallaig). Turn right at the **B8004** to the Caledonian Canal's locks at Banavie, 4 miles (6km).*

RECOMMENDED WALKS

There are good walks to be enjoyed in this area and local tourist information centres have guidebooks giving details of many of them. Glen Nevis, which is below Ben Nevis and easily reached from Fort William, provides a walk with waterfalls to see on the way. The Caledonian Canal's footpath provides good level walking for families.

❶ Banavie, Highland

Northeast of Fort William, on the way to Banavie, are the impressive ruins of 13th-century Inverlochy Castle, on the banks of the River Lochy. It has massive round towers at the corners and walls 10-feet (3m) thick.

The Caledonian Canal runs through the Great Glen from Corpach (just southwest of Banavie) to Inverness, a total distance of 60 miles (97km). It was built between 1803 and 1822 by Thomas Telford so that boats could avoid the treacherous waters round Cape Wrath; the political decision to build the canal was hastened by the government's fear of Napoleon's naval strength. Although some commercial boats still use this beautifully sited waterway, most of the craft on it are motor cruisers or yachts and their passage through the locks is always of interest to land-lubbers. Neptune's Staircase, the most spectacular part of the canal, is found at Banavie. This is a series of eight locks that raise boats a total height of 64 feet (20m) in a distance of only 1,500 feet (460m).

A short walk along the towpath leads to the basin and sea lock at Corpach; the neat 'pepper pot' lighthouse is a delightful structure. From this point there is an excellent view of Loch Linnhe and the surrounding hills. This is probably one of the best places from which to see Ben Nevis.

▶ *Return to the **A830**. Turn right and follow the road to Glenfinnan.*

❷ Glenfinnan, Highland

On the fateful afternoon of 19 August 1745, Charles Edward Stuart raised the Stuart standard here and rallied more than a thousand armed supporters to the Jacobite cause. His father was proclaimed King James VIII of Scotland and III of England and Ireland and this historic

BACK TO NATURE

The grandeur of the scenery derives from the area's fascinating geology and the Great Glen Fault that runs right through the Highlands along a line joining Fort William and Inverness. Loch Linnhe and the Caledonian Canal lie along this great gash in the earth's surface, produced as the two sides of the glen moved past each other. The very occasional earth tremors indicate that the fault has not yet stopped moving!

Steam train crossing the Glenfinnan viaduct

event started the tragic chain of events known in Scots history as the 'Forty-Five'. The army, though initially successful in moving far into England, was eventually defeated at Culloden, near Inverness, on 16 April 1746, a defeat that did much to change the history of Scotland. The NTS Visitor Centre has a good display explaining the events surrounding the arrival of the prince and the raising of the standard. The nearby tall and slender monument at the head of Loch Shiel is Scotland's most famous memorial to the Jacobite cause.

The Fort William to Mallaig road runs parallel to the railway line for much of the way. The line's most spectacular structure is the Glenfinnan Viaduct with its 21 arches; the local railway station has a little museum depicting the history of the line.

i *NTS Visitor Centre (seasonal)*

▶ *Follow the **A830** for 14 miles (23km) to Loch nan Uamh.*

8 **Loch nan Uamh,** Highland

After the battle of Culloden, Bonnie Prince Charlie made his way back to this area and, on 20 September 1746, he sailed away from this loch on a ship bound for France. The spot from which he sailed is marked by the 'Prince's Cairn'. He had a price of £30,000 on his head but no one betrayed his presence while on the run from government troops, so loyal were local people to the Jacobite cause.

▶ *Continue on the **A830** to Arisaig.*

4 **Arisaig,** Highland

This little seaside village has many sandy beaches nearby which makes it popular with families in summer. Arisaig has a fine view of the islands of Rum and Eigg and boats sail from the small harbour to these and other local islands.

▶ *Continue on the **A830** to Morar.*

The Prince's Cairn at Loch nan Uamh

5 **Morar,** Highland

Loch Morar, with a depth of 1,017 feet (310m) is Britain's deepest inland water and the home of Morag, a 'monster' reputed to be related to Loch Ness' Nessie. The loch is a

---

FOR CHILDREN

Of the many fine beaches along this coast, particular mention should be made of the ones at Morar, north of Arisaig, and at Kentra Bay. There are not many wet-weather facilities in the area, but Fort William has the Lochaber Leisure Centre which has a swimming pool and facilities for many sports including outdoor activities such as tennis.
There are also dry-ski slopes at the skiing area at Aonach Mor, just off the A82, east of Fort William

As the A861 descends to Acharacle, it passes a minor road (left) to Dalelia and this leads to a walk to the shores of Loch Shiel. This is the narrowest part of the loch and is almost completely blocked by Eilean Fhianain (St Finnan's Island), where St Finnan, a disciple of St Columba, built a chapel. The ruins survive, and legend has it that a curse has been placed on anyone daring to remove the bell Finnan brought from Ireland. The churchyard was the burial place of the chiefs of Clanranald. This was also the spot from which Charles Edward Stuart started his journey up Loch Shiel to Glenfinnan where he raised the Stuart standard in 1745.

for a wide expanse of pure white silica sand.

▶ *Continue on the **A830** to Mallaig.*

⑥ Mallaig, Highland
Before the arrival of the railway, Mallaig was a small crofting community with a few thatched houses. Today it is the home port of a substantial fishing fleet, host to the Marine World Aquarium down by the harbour, and a heritage centre by the station, as well as being the mainland terminal for many boats operating ferry services to the islands.

Day excursions from the harbour are also available in season and these give visitors the opportunity to visit Skye or Muck, Eigg, Rum and Canna.

A landed catch of mixed shellfish

The peninsula of Knoydart is another fascinating place accessible only by boat. Surrounded on three sides by sea and on the fourth by mountains, it is one of Scotland's few wilderness areas; it retains its character because it cannot be reached by road. This is wonderful walking country, where real peace and quiet can be enjoyed.

The West Highland Railway from Fort William was opened in 1894 in order to transport the west coast herring catches to the southern markets as quickly as possible, and although the fish-carrying role

Fishing boats in Mallaig's pretty harbour

remarkable example of the effect of glaciers during the Ice Age. The ice here was 4,000 feet (1,220m) thick and gouged out the loch's basin to a depth of more than 1,000 feet (300m) below sea level.

After tumbling over the Falls of Morar, the River Morar flows over the Sands of Morar, notable

of the line has diminished, it is still of vital economic and social importance to the area. It is also very popular with summer visitors, especially when steam trains are used, and it has been described as one of the world's most scenic railway journeys.

SCENIC ROUTES

The 'Road to the Isles' is the name given to the attractive route from Fort William to Mallaig, which passes through an ever-changing landscape of hills, forest and lochs. Another outstanding journey is the one along Loch Linnhe, giving good views of Ben Nevis and the hills of Glen Coe.

▶ *Return along the **A830** to Lochailort. Turn right at the **A861** and follow to Kinlochmoidart.*

⑦ Kinlochmoidart,
Highland
To the right of the road stand the 'Seven Men of Moidart', seven beech trees planted early in the 19th century in tribute to the seven men who landed here with Bonnie Prince Charlie in 1745. The area around Loch Moidart is beautifully wooded with a large natural oak and birch forest; holly, cherry and ash are also common. Today these trees are protected, but in previous centuries they were used for charcoal burning or for making lime. An old lime kiln stands opposite the car-park at the 'Seven Men of Moidart'. After climbing out of Kinlochmoidart, look out for a group of four cairns by the roadside. These are on an old 'coffin route' and mark where coffins were laid to give their bearers a rest while carrying their burden over the trackless hills to the local churchyard.

▶ *Continue on the **A861** for 7 miles (11km) to Acharacle.*

⑧ Acharacle, Highland
This small village, which makes a pleasant base from which to explore the surrounding area, is approached by crossing the Old Shiel Bridge.

To the west lies Kentra Bay with its fine sandy beaches, and Castle Tioram, a 14th-century castle standing on a tidal island in Loch Moidart. Though an empty ruin, it was not destroyed in battle, but put to the torch by its owner, the chief of Clanranald, during the 1715 Jacobite uprising. He did this to prevent it falling into the hands of his enemies.

▶ *Continue on the **A861** to Salen, then turn right at the **B8007** and follow it to Glenmore.*

⑨ Glenmore, Highland
Excellent displays on the local landscape and wildlife can be

The remains of tragic Tioram Castle

seen at the Ardnamurchan Natural History Visitor Centre here. Further along the road is the little bay of Camas nan Geall beneath the steep slopes of Ben Hiant. In the field at the back of the bay can be found an 18th-century burial site and a Bronze Age standing stone which has a number of carvings on it; the remains of a small settlement can also be seen here.

▶ *Continue on the **B8007** for 11 miles (18km) to Kilchoan.*

⑩ Kilchoan, Highland
This little settlement of scattered houses makes a good base for exploring the western end of the Ardnamurchan peninsula; it also has a summer season ferry service to Tobermory on the

island of Mull. Close to the settlement stands 13th-century Mingary Castle. This was originally the seat of the MacIains and later the Campbells of Ardnamurchan, who held it for the king during the Jacobite rising in 1745.

Beyond Kilchoan is Ardnamurchan Point, the most westerly point on the British mainland. The view from here encompasses the Inner Hebrides and the islands of Barra and South Uist. Its lighthouse was built in the 1840s by Alan Stevenson, one of the three Stevenson brothers who followed their father in designing lighthouses. The building is constructed of pink granite from the Ross of Mull and the design was influenced by Egyptian architecture.

i Kilchoan (seasonal)

▶ *Return to Salen along the B8007, then turn right at the A861 to Strontian.*

11 Strontian, Highland
The modern portion of this village lies near the main road while the older part is to be found on the western side of the Strontian river. From 1722 to 1904, this was the site of mines extracting lead, zinc and silver but the most lasting contribution the village gave to science was through the discovery here in 1764 of the mineral strontianite. The examination of this mineral led to the discovery of the metal element strontium, used in fireworks. Its radioisotope, Strontium 90, is used in nuclear power sources. The former mining area is now a source of barytes, which is used in drillers' 'mud' as a lubricating agent for the

drilling mechanism on North Sea oil rigs.

Ariundle Oakwood nature reserve lies to the north of the Strontian river and has a collection of fine oaks and Scots pines. A pleasant nature trail can be followed through the reserve.

i Strontian (seasonal)

▶ *Continue on the A861, then turn right at the A884. Follow this to Loch Aline and then continue to the village of Lochaline.*

12 Lochaline, Highland
Peaceful Loch Aline, which slices into the broad peninsula of Morvern, seems a rather incongruous place to have a modern mine, but close to the village is a source of very pure silica sand which is used in the production of high quality glassware. Behind the village, in the graveyard of Keil Church, stands a tall 15th-century Celtic cross, known as the Morvern Cross. Lochaline has a ferry service to Fishnish on Mull. At the head of the loch stand Kinlochaline Castle and Ardtornish House, which has extensive gardens, well worth visiting. To the south of the mansion stands 14th-

century Ardtornish Castle, an imposing building on the coast that still acts as an important landmark to sailors travelling down through the Sound of Mull.

▶ *Return on the A884 to the junction (right) with the B8043. Cars should follow this unclassified road until the A861 is met and then turn right and follow this road to Ardgour. Vehicles pulling caravans should avoid the B8043 and instead continue on the A884 to its junction with the A861; then turn right to Ardgour.*

13 Ardgour, Highland
The small village of Ardgour has developed at this important crossing over Loch Linnhe. The old jetty here was built by Thomas Telford in 1815, at about the same time as the lighthouse, which still acts as a prominant landmark.

▶ *Take the Corran ferry across Loch Linnhe at the Corran Narrows. At the other side turn left at the A82 and return to Fort William, 8 miles (13km).*

The distinctive landmark of Ardgour lighthouse and Corran ferry on Loch Linnhe

The Western
Highlands

The fort at Fort Augustus, built by General Wade in 1730, was named after William Augustus, Duke of Cumberland who brutally supressed the Highlanders after the Battle of Culloden in 1746. In 1867 the fort became a Benedictine school; today it is a heritage centre, and Fort Augustus is a popular base for cruisers on the Caledonian Canal.

3 DAYS • 301 MILES • 484 KM

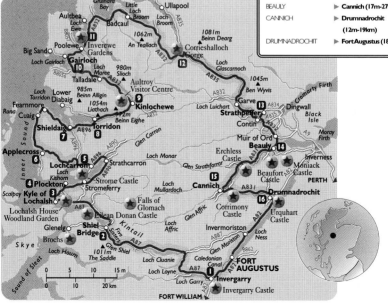

ⓘ Car Park (seasonal)

▶ *Head southwards on the* **A82** *for 7 miles (11km) to Invergarry.*

❶ Invergarry, Highland
This rather sleepy-looking village was the home of an important clan, the MacDonnells of Glengarry. To the south lie the ruins of Invergarry Castle; three castles have stood here, the last one having been burnt in 1746 by Cumberland because Charles Edward Stuart stayed here before and after the battle of Culloden. Just to the north of Invergarry stands the roadside Well of Seven Heads, a gruesome reminder of the slaying of seven MacDonnell brothers who had murdered their dead brother's two sons. The story of this gory event is recorded on a monument inscribed in Gaelic, English, Latin and French.

▶ *Leave by the* **A87** *(to Kyle of Lochalsh) and follow this for 36 miles (58km) to Shiel Bridge.*

❷ Shiel Bridge, Highland
The imposing entry to Shiel Bridge is by the magnificent Glen Shiel, on whose north side is the group of mountains known as the Five Sisters of Kintail. The mountains are seen to great advantage at Mam Ratagan, just a little to the west of Invershiel on the Glenelg road. Like many communities in this region, Shiel Bridge is a collection of houses at an important junction, in this case at the head of Loch Duich. Along the northern shore of the loch stands Eilean Donan Castle, whose foundations date back to 1220. Shelled by a British frigate in 1719 during an abortive Jacobite rising, it lay in ruins until rebuilding started in 1912. It is now one of the Highlands' most popular and beautiful castles and is said to be the most photographed castle in Scotland.
There is an unmanned NTS

centre at Strath Croe, to the northeast of Shiel Bridge, with useful wildlife displays explaining the natural history of this wild and beautiful area. A very rough cross-country path from Strath Croe leads to the Falls of Glomach where the water of the Allt a' Ghlomaich tumbles 750 feet (230m).

ⓘ Shiel Bridge (seasonal); NTS, Strath Croe

▶ *Continue on the* **A87** *for 15 miles (24km) to Kyle of Lochalsh.*

❸ Kyle of Lochalsh, Highland
This bustling industrial village is the terminus of the railway line from Inverness. The new (and controversial) bridge that replaced the Skye ferries is reached by the A87. The western part of this peninsula lies within the NTS's Balmacara estate; 1 mile (1.5km) beyond the village of Reraig, Lochalsh House Woodland Garden is on the left. This boasts a fine

Eilean Donan Castle, resurrected from the rubble in 1912

collection of mature trees, and is developing more exotic species of plants such as bamboo trees.

ⓘ Car Park, Kyle of Lochalsh (seasonal)

FOR HISTORY BUFFS

To the west of Shiel Bridge lies Glenelg. The route to it has long been of strategic importance, hence the 18th-century military road and the (ruined) Bernera Barracks. It was used by Samuel Johnson and James Boswell in 1773 and is now followed by many summer visitors heading for the Kyle Rhea ferry to Skye. South of the village are two brochs, Dun Telve and Dun Trodden, built as defensive structures about 2,000 years ago, when they were over 40 feet (13m) high and had stairs and galleries built into their walls.

▶ *Leave by the unclassified road that leads northwards to Plockton.*

4 Plockton, Highland
With palm trees growing by the shore of Loch Carron, Plockton exudes the kind of peace and quiet that has attracted generations of painters; indeed, many would regard it as one of the northwest coast's loveliest villages. The sheltered position also provides a much-needed haven for yachts sailing along the west coast.

▶ *Return along the approach road to Plockton and turn left to head eastwards towards Stromeferry, following the shore of Loch Carron. Turn left when the **A890** is met. Follow to just beyond Strathcarron railway station then turn left on to the **A896** to Lochcarron.*

5 Lochcarron, Highland
Lochcarron is essentially a long string of houses (and a few hotels) along the shore of the sea loch. To its south is Strome Castle, once a stronghold of the MacDonnells of Glengarry, but destroyed by the MacKenzies in 1602. It commands a fine view of Skye. Just west of the village is Loch Kishorn, a deep and sheltered loch where enormous North Sea oil rigs were once built.

⃞ *Main Street (seasonal)*

▶ *Continue on the **A896** but turn left at the head of Loch Kishorn to Applecross. This road is definitely not for caravans, but the **A896** from Loch Kishorn to Shieldaig and the minor road from Shieldaig to Applecross are suitable.*

6 Applecross, Highland
Applecross was one of the country's most isolated communities until the coastal road from Shieldaig was built in the 1970s. The traditional route, over the 2,053-foot (626m) pass of Bealach na Ba (Pass of the

Cattle), one of the highest roads in Britain, was a formidable obstacle to many vehicles and it is often closed by snow in winter.

An Irish monk, Maelrubha, landed at Applecross in the AD670s and founded a monastery which was later destroyed by Vikings. The local church has an ancient cross slab 9 feet (3m) high, with a Celtic cross inscribed. This and others inside the church may date back to Maelrubha's time. An old chapel stands in the graveyard and two rounded stones in front of it mark the resting place of Maelrubha.

▶ *Head north on the unclassified road out of Applecross to Shieldaig. Turn left at the **A896**, then bear left to enter Shieldaig.*

7 Shieldaig, Highland
This charming village consists of a row of whitewashed houses standing along the loch's shore. Once famous for its herring fishing (its name is Norse for 'herring bay'), it now relies more on tourism to maintain its livelihood. Opposite the harbour lies the small wooded Shieldaig Island. From around Shieldaig there are wonderful views of some of the Highlands' best scenery. The mountains from Loch Kishorn northwards to Loch Maree are composed of red Torridonian sandstone, some 750 millions years old. However, around Shieldaig the rocks are a highly altered variety called gneiss which has been eroded to provide a low, smooth, platform above which the giant Torridon mountains soar.

▶ *Continue on the **A896** for 8 miles (13km) to Torridon.*

8 Torridon, Highland
The houses huddled together in the village are dwarfed by the mass of 3,456-foot (1,054m) Liathach, a mountain to be attempted only by experienced mountainwalkers as its ridge is very narrow and exposed. Composed of Torridonian sandstone, its name means the Grey

Sitting on the top of the world, looking north to Torridon village

One, as four of its seven tops are formed from grey-white quartzite rock.

An NTS countryside centre is situated just by the main road and this has displays and audio-visual presentations on the local geology and wildlife. Near by, there is a small Deer Museum; many breeds of deer may be spotted near here and can even be found wandering around the village itself.

RECOMMENDED WALKS

A low-level walk runs behind Liathach, with a detour to the corrie north of Ben Eighe, Coire Mhic Fhearchair, which has three buttresses towering over a lochan (small loch). Take care, as this is very exposed country and 'casual' walkers should not attempt it.

i NTS Centre (seasonal)

▶ *Follow the A896 for 11 miles (18km) to Kinlochewe.*

9 Kinlochewe, Highland
This village stands at the head of Loch Maree, which was once called Loch Ewe, hence the name of the village. To its west

lies the Beinn Eighe National Nature Reserve and the reserve's Aultroy Visitor Centre is just along the A832 from the village. Further on is an interesting nature trail which climbs to a fine view over the loch towards Slioch, the 3,217-foot (980m) high mountain that dominates the surrounding district. Loch Maree is one of the country's finest lochs and is steeped in history. The tiny Isle Maree was once a sacred place of the Druids, who are said to have introduced oak trees, one of their religious symbols. In the 7th century, St Maelrubha came and set up his cell here and, for similar reasons, planted holly trees. In later centuries, paganism was practised here and rites involving the sacrifice of a bull occurred on the island as late as the 17th century. The Loch Maree Hotel has a large boulder outside it on which is a Gaelic inscription celebrating a visit by Queen Victoria; a translation is above the hotel's entrance.

▶ *Leave Kinlochewe on the A832 for 20 miles (32km) to Gairloch.*

10 Gairloch, Highland
This widely scattered crofting and fishing community is the district's main centre and it has developed into a popular place for holidays as it combines fine scenery with long stretches of sandy beach. Fishing is important here and the harbour is well worth visiting when the boats come in. The fishing industry, crofting and other aspects of local life form important displays at the local Gairloch

Exotic and more common plants at Inverewe Gardens

FOR CHILDREN

Gairloch has some of the best beaches in the western Highlands. As well as the beach at the village, there are good ones relatively near by, at Big Sand (to the west) and Red Point (further away to the southwest). For wet-weather activity, there is a swimming pool at Poolewe. The Gairloch Centre has facilities for sports as diverse as climbing, archery, badminton and short tennis. These are some of the few indoor activities for children in the region, something that may have to be considered if the weather is bad.

Heritage Museum which was developed from a farmstead with a cobbled courtyard.

☐ *Auchtercairn*

▶ *Continue on the A832 to Inverewe Gardens, just beyond the village of Poolewe.*

🇮🇮 Inverewe Gardens, Highland

In 1862 Osgood MacKenzie started a long labour of love when he began transforming an area of barren ground here into one of Britain's most remarkable gardens. Conifers were planted to form shelter belts, wet land was drained, soil was carried in on men's backs and in 60 years, the local people had created a garden that gives great pleasure to over 100,000 visitors each year. Inverewe lies at the same latitude as Siberia, but here, bathed by the warm Gulf Stream, it boasts palms, magnolias, hydrangeas, rhododendrons and many other plants.

On a summer's day Loch Ewe is a peaceful place, a far cry from the days of World War II when it was a convoy station for ships bound for Russia or Iceland. Aultbea (a little further along the road) was the depot's HQ and remains of gun emplacements have been kept as reminders of the district's role in those dangerous days. Look out for information boards near Aultbea's pier.

☐ *NTS Centre Inverewe*

▶ *Continue on the A832 to the A835. Turn left and continue for less than a mile (1.5km).*

🇮🇩 Corrieshalloch Gorge, Highland

Much of the Highland landscape was sculpted by the movement of ice during the last Ice Age. Often the ice smoothed the land, but at Corrieshalloch Gorge its meltwater flowing down the River Broom gouged out this spectacular rugged gorge about one mile (1.5km) long. A narrow bridge crosses the chasm with the water plunging over the Falls of Measach some 150 feet (45m) below – this is not the place for vertigo sufferers! The bridge was built by Sir John Fowler, joint designer of the Forth Rail Bridge, but this is hardly on the same scale and there is a limit to the number of people permitted on the bridge at one time.

The busy fishing port of Ullapool lies further down Loch Broom. This bustling little village was founded in 1788 by the British Fisheries Society to take advantage of the huge shoals of herring found in the nearby seas. It is an important ferry terminal for Stornoway; cruises to the Summer Isles are also available from the harbour.

▶ *Head southeast on the A835 towards Inverness. Turn left at Contin on to the A834 to Strathpeffer.*

🇮🇩 Strathpeffer, Highland

Strathpeffer prospered as a spa in the 19th century after springs (four sulphur and one chalybeate) were developed. The Victorian hotels and large villas date from the spa's heyday and today the hotels still do a brisk trade, catering mainly for bus tours. The spa water can be sampled in a small building by the Square but beware – its taste is even more pungent than its smell! Local handicrafts can be bought at the small shops now occupying the old railway station buildings.

At the northern end of the village is the Eagle Stone, a Pictish stone also said to celebrate a victory of the Munros over the MacDonalds. To the east, the prominent hill of Knockfarrel affords fine views over the district.

☐ *The Square (seasonal)*

▶ *Return along the A834 to the A835 and turn left. Turn right at the A832 and at Muir of Ord take the A862 southwards to Beauly.*

🇮🇩 Beauly, Highland

Mary, Queen of Scots is supposed to have come here in 1564 and taken a liking to the place; tradition has it she described it as a 'bèau lieu' (beautiful place), hence its name. However, it is more likely Beauly derives from the name given to the 13th-century priory around which the town was built. Beauly Priory was founded in 1230 and the present ruins date from the 13th to the 16th centuries. In 1572 Lord Ruthven obtained royal permission to strip the lead off the roof and by 1633 the building was in a ruinous condition. The town's 'modern' planned layout (built around 1840) features a wide market square and a grid street pattern.

There are many castles in the area. To the southeast is Moniack Castle, which makes wine from local produce; to the south is Beaufort Castle, built about 1880 in Scots baronial style; and near the road to Cannich stands Erchless Castle, described in the 19th century as 'modernised, yet still a stately old pile'.

▶ *Leave on the A862 (to Inverness) and turn right at the A831 and continue to Cannich.*

Brooding Urquhart Castle

15 Cannich, Highland
Cannich stands at the head of Strathglass, a glen not normally on tourist routes. The lower part of the glen has an impressive narrow gorge (at An Druim) and there are a number of hydro-electric power stations here.

To the west of Cannich lie some very beautiful glens – Glen Affric, Glen Cannich and Glen Strathfarrar. These make for good walks as the scenery can be spectacularly wild in places: Scots pines are being regenerated and there are chances of seeing red deer. Corrimony Cairn is found just off the Cannich to Drumnadrochit road. This is about 4,000 years old and has a central grave chamber which can be reached by crawling through the passageway. Standing stones ring the cairn and the large capstone lying on top of it has small circular indentations called 'cup marks' on it. Further along this narrow road, the standing stone known as Mony's Stone can be found, as well as the walled rectangular graveyard of Clach Churadain (St Curadan's Cemetery).

▶ Continue on the **A831** for 12 miles (19km) to Drumnadrochit.

Loch Ness's most famous resident

16 Drumnadrochit,
Highland
Huge numbers of visitors come here hoping to see Loch Ness monster. The loch is only 2 miles (3km) wide at this point but about 750 feet (230m) deep and many 'sightings' have been reported. In the AD600s, St Adamnan told how Columba drove back a monster when it was about to attack a swimmer. Frequent scientific expeditions have attempted to find her, but there is still no definite proof that a monster exists; however, even sceptical visitors should keep a loaded camera handy! The Loch Ness Centre in Drumnadrochit has exhibits connected with Nessie, including possible photographs of the beast herself.

Just outside the village stands Urquhart Castle. The site may have been fortified in the Dark Ages but the present structure dates back to the 13th century. Its commanding position in the Great Glen gave it immense military importance and part of it was blown up in the late 17th century to prevent it falling into the hands of Jacobites. Further south, the road passes a cairn erected to John Cobb who died on the

loch in 1952 while attempting to set a new world speed record; he achieved the remarkable speed of 206mph (331kph) before the accident.

The village of Foyers can be seen on the opposite shore of the loch. In 1896, Britain's first major commercial hydroelectric power station was built here to provide energy for an aluminium works. These buildings can still be seen though the factory has long since closed. Today, a large pump-storage scheme produces electricity using the water of Loch Mhor, which is on the moorland above the village.

▶ Head south on the **A82** and return to Fort Augustus.

SCENIC ROUTES

As a detour, the narrow and twisty road from Torridon to Lower Diabaig is highly recommended as there are splendid views of Loch Torridon. In addition, the small picturesque lochside settlements of Inveralligin and Lower Diabaig are worth seeing.

The Wild
West

This tour really does reveal the wide, wild expanse of the Highlands landscape. It begins at Bonar Bridge, named after the first bridge to be built over the Kyle of Sutherland at this point, designed by Thomas Telford but later destroyed by a flood. The village at Ardgay lies on the other side of the bridge.

2 DAYS • 277KM • 172 MILES

ITINERARY		
BONAR BRIDGE	▶	**Knockan Cliff**
		(36m-58km)
KNOCKAN CLIFF	▶	**Inchnadamph**
		(11m-18km)
INCHNADAMPH	▶	**Lochinver (13m-21km)**
LOCHINVER	▶	**Kylesku (27m-43km)**
KYLESKU	▶	**Scourie (12m-19km)**
SCOURIE	▶	**Kinlochbervie**
		(16m-26km)
KINLOCHBERVIE	▶	**Lairg (46m-74km)**
LAIRG	▶	**Bonar Bridge (11m-18km)**

Inverpolly National Nature Reserve, as viewed from Cul Mor

FOR HISTORY BUFFS

To the west of Bonar Bridge, a narrow road leads through Strathcarron to Croick Church. This was designed by Thomas Telford in 1827 for what was then a well-populated district. However, in 1845, during the infamous Clearances, the landowner tried to evict the people. Three attempts were made to throw the 18 families out of their homes and eventually they were forced to gather at this church with only a few possessions. They stayed there for a week, sheltering under blankets, and recorded their plight by scratching messages on the church's window panes.

▶ *Leave by the A836 and turn left at the A837. Continue on this to Ledmore Junction, then turn left on to the A835 to the Nature Trail at Knockan Cliff.*

FOR CHILDREN

As an unusual treat, why not spend a night in a castle? Carbisdale Castle is now used to house a youth hostel, complete with statues, paintings and beautiful wood-work, and will delight many children.

❶ Knockan Cliff, Highland
The geological trail at Knockan Cliff provides a wonderful view of the district's unique landscape. Tall and isolated sandstone mountains rise steeply from the boggy moorland which is based on the very old rock known as Lewisian gneiss. This wilderness is part of the Inverpolly National Nature Reserve and its visitor centre gives an invaluable introduction to this strange and fascinating landscape. The walks are spectacular, but only for prepared and experienced walkers. At

one point on the trail, you can stand beside the world-famous Moine Thrust where a huge slab of land (running from Loch Eriboll on the north coast all the way to the island of Islay) moved many miles westward, resulting in the geologically older rock coming to rest on the younger rock.

Much of Inverpolly is covered with wet heath, its main plants being heather, cottongrass and deergrass. The myriad boggy areas and little pools give shelter to bog myrtle and unusual plants such as the carnivorous sundew. Deer roam the land, spending summer in the high corries, but moving down to sheltered places during the winter. Otters, wild cats, pine martens and badgers can also be seen in the district. In good weather, this is the

The ruins of Ardvreck Castle on the shores of Loch Assynt

Highlands at its best; in bad weather, you won't see anything!

▶ *Return along the **A835** to Ledmore Junction. Turn left at the **A837** and follow this to Inchnadamph, 11 miles (18km).*

2 Inchnadamph, Highland
A hotel and a few houses stand near the road at the Inchnadamph Nature Reserve in an area popular with anglers. This is limestone country and the Allt nan Uamh caves near the valley of the River Traligill were used by late Stone Age people. Some of the earliest traces of people living in Scotland have been found here, presumably attracted by the better soil and the 'ready-made' houses. Near the roadside houses, a cairn stands as a memorial to the two geologists, Benjamin Peach and John

Horne, who unravelled the mysteries of the local landscape. Beyond the settlement lies Loch Assynt, its dark pine-clad islands in stark contrast to the grassy hillsides. By its shore stands the ruin of Ardvreck Castle. In 1650 the Marquis of Montrose (well known for his exploits against the Covenanters, religious dissenters) fled here. Neil Macleod imprisoned him and dispatched him to Edinburgh to be barbarously hanged, drawn and quartered. Although Macleod expected a bounty of £20,000 for Montrose, he was paid in oatmeal – 56,000 pounds (25,000kg) of it!

Calda House, which stands near the castle, was built in 1695 but was burned to the ground in somewhat mysterious circumstances in 1737.

▶ *Continue on the **A837** for 13 miles (21km) to Lochinver.*

❸ **Lochinver,** Highland

This is Assynt's main village and an important fishing port specialising in whitefish and shellfish. The life and history of the area is told in the village's Assynt Visitor Centre.

During the summer it is popular with visitors, walkers and fishermen. A local place of interest is the Highland Stoneware factory which produces many types of high quality hand-painted pottery.

From north of Lochinver, there are magnificent views of Suilven, at 2,399 feet (731m), one of Britain's most spectacularly shaped mountains. From this direction it rises as a huge dome of reddish-brown sandstone above the platform of the much lighter-coloured gneiss. The Vikings called it Sul Fhal, the Pillar Mountain, but the Gaelic name is Caisteal Liath,

The tranquil harbour of Lochinver

the Grey Castle. It is regarded by many Scots as one of the country's most attractive hills; however, it is not one of the district's most-climbed hills as the moorland walk-in – although enjoyable – is quite long.

[i] *Main Street (seasonal)*

▶ *Leave by the **A837** and turn*

FOR CHILDREN

The area north of Lochinver has some wonderful sandy beaches, many of which can be relatively quiet even at the height of summer. Some of the best-known ones are at Achmelvich, Clachtoll and Clashnessie, all of which have sheltered bays and very clean beaches.

Crated local fish ready for export

left at the B869. Continue on this road to the A894, then turn left to reach the bridge at Kylesku. The B869 is a narrow twisting road with many steep hills and it is unsuitable for caravans. An alternative route for caravans is the A837 from Lochinver to Skiag Bridge and then left at the A894.

4 Kylesku, Highland
The Kylesku bridge, a graceful concrete construction that has won many accolades, crosses Loch a' Chàirn Bhàin with a view towards the pointed peak of Quinag which dominates the southern shore. To the east, the loch splits into two arms and boat trips are available on Loch Glencoul to visit seals and herons and to get a view of the remote waterfall Eas-Coul-Aulin. This is Britain's highest waterfall at over 650 feet (200m) high.

The car-park on the northern side of the bridge offers excellent views of Quinag, the huge mountain that lies between Kylesku and Loch Assynt. It has seven peaks, the highest being 2,653 feet (808m). Like many of the neighbouring hills, it has a base of gneiss, but for the most part is sandstone; a few of the peaks have quartzite caps. Its name comes from the Gaelic Cuinneag, meaning a churn or pail.

▶ *Continue on the A894 for 12 miles (19km) to Scourie.*

5 Scourie, Highland
This crofting community nestles comfortably in a sheltered hollow. It is a popular centre from which to tour the district and many walkers, fishermen and other visitors find this a charming base. Despite its northerly position, palm trees grow in the garden of Scourie Lodge. The local landscape has earned the description 'knob and lochan' (a lochan is a small loch) as the undulating gneiss landscape is studded with little hillocks and countless pools. Where peat bogs have developed, these are used as a source of fuel and many of the villagers

The Kylesku Bridge spanning Loch a' Chàirn Bhàin

Crofters' cottages in Scourie, where a more traditional way of life still persists

stacking them to dry before taking them home for the winter.

To the north is Loch Laxford, a haven for seabirds and seals. Summer cruises on the loch are available from Fanagmore.

BACK TO NATURE

The rocks in the Scourie and Laxford area are some of the oldest in Europe and may date back over 2,700 million years. They have undergone many changes and some indication of the complexity of the folding and flow of the rocks can be seen at the massive road cuttings at Laxford Brae, just after the A838 leaves Loch Laxford.

▶ Continue on the **A894** to Laxford Bridge and turn left at the **A838**. Turn left at the **B801** which ends at Kinlochbervie, a distance of 16 miles (26km).

6 **Kinlochbervie,** Highland

In the 1960s this crofting village began its transformation into one of Scotland's most important modern harbours. Nowadays many boats, a large proportion of them originally from the more traditional fishing ports of the east coast of Scotland, land substantial catches of cod, haddock, whiting and many other varieties here.

The minor road beyond Kinlochbervie leads to the little community of Sheigra, passing glorious coastal scenery at crofting townships such as Oldshoremore (where there is also a superb beach). The 13th-century manuscript of the Haakon Saga records the fact that King Haakon anchored at Oldshoremore in 1263 when he commenced his invasion of Scotland.

The view to the east is dominated by the impressive hills of Ben Stack, Arkle and Foinaven.

▶ Return along the **B801** and the **A838** to Laxford Bridge and turn to the left. Continue along the **A838**, then turn right at the **A836** to reach Lairg.

7 **Lairg,** Highland

Lairg was established beside the River Shin in one of the few areas of decent arable land in Sutherland. This district was once quite well populated, but after the Clearances many of the displaced people emigrated to America or the British colonies. The Ferrycroft Countryside Centre features the history and archaeology of the area. Further down the river are the Falls of Shin with a summer season visitor centre. This is a good salmon river and fish must climb the falls in order to return to their spawning grounds upstream. In days of old, poachers used to come to the falls and either spear or shoot the fish as they attempted to leap the falls.

i Ferrycroft Countryside Centre (seasonal)

A tapestry depicting the notorious Highland Clearances of the 18th century

▶ Leave by the **A836** and follow it back to Bonar Bridge.

RECOMMENDED WALKS

Try the walk to Sandwood Bay: the path starts at Blairmore between Oldshoremore and Sheigra. Sandwood Bay has a ghost – a 'bearded sailor' – and mermaids are said to have been seen here!

Northern
Highlights

This tour traces the most northerly point of Scotland, visiting many wide, sandy – and largely empty – beaches. Dornoch is its starting point, with a fine bay and championship golf course. Its attractiveness is enhanced by its sandstone buildings and a spacious centre dominated by the cathedral.

2/3 DAYS • 433KM • 269 MILES

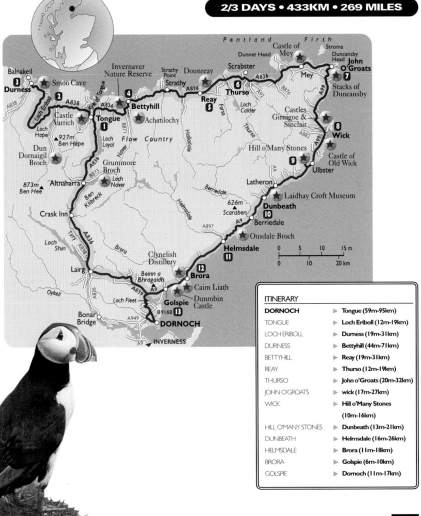

ITINERARY

DORNOCH	▶	Tongue (59m-95km)
TONGUE	▶	Loch Eriboll (12m-19km)
LOCH ERIBOLL	▶	Durness (19m-31km)
DURNESS	▶	Bettyhill (44m-71km)
BETTYHILL	▶	Reay (19m-31km)
REAY	▶	Thurso (12m-19km)
THURSO	▶	John o'Groats (20m-32km)
JOHN O'GROATS	▶	wick (17m-27km)
WICK	▶	Hill o'Many Stones
		(10m-16km)
HILL O'MANY STONES	▶	Dunbeath (13m-21km)
DUNBEATH	▶	Helmsdale (16m-26km)
HELMSDALE	▶	Brora (11m-18km)
BRORA	▶	Golspie (6m-10km)
GOLSPIE	▶	Dornoch (11m-17km)

▶ Leave by the **A949** and turn right when the **A9** is met. Turn left at the **A839** and follow it to Lairg. Leave Lairg by the **A836** and follow it to Tongue.

❶ Tongue, Highland
Tongue occupies a marvellous position overlooking the wide sandy estuary of the Kyle of Tongue. To the west of the village stands the ruin of Castle Varrich, or Caisteal Bharraich, a 14th-century stronghold of the MacKays on a site that may have been used by an 11th-century Norse king. Nearby Tongue House used to be the home of the chiefs of the MacKay clan.

▶ Leave by the **A838** and follow it for 12 miles (19km) to Loch Eriboll.

❷ Loch Eriboll, Highland
This is one of the north coast's deepest and most sheltered sea lochs and it was used during World War II by convoys of ships waiting to sail across the North Atlantic. The sailors knew this rather desolate place as 'Loch 'Orrible'!

On the eastern side of the loch, a spit runs out to the rocky promontory of Ard Neackie on which are the very substantial remains of four lime kilns which were constructed around 1870.

▶ Continue on the **A838** for 19 miles (31km) to Durness.

❸ Durness, Highland
A popular stopping point for visitors, not only for the local scenery, but also for the huge expanses of sandy beaches at the village and at neighbouring Balnakeil.

The wide, sandy estuary of the Kyle of Tongue

Durness is situated in a limestone area and is best known for Smoo Cave. The main cavern is huge – about 200 feet (60m) long and 110 feet (35m) wide and is easy to enter. Beyond this, a second cave has a 'swallow hole' in its roof and a stream, the Allt Smoo, tumbles 80 feet (25m) into it. A third cave can only be entered by boat. To the west of the village lies beautiful Balnakeil Bay which has a wide sweep of sand backed by tall grass-covered dunes. The site of the ruined church nearby may date back to the 8th century when St Maelrubha of Applecross was in this district. The southern wall of the church contains the tomb of the murdered Donald MacLeod, reckoned to be

BACK TO NATURE

While the attention of most visitors will be focused on the coast, the landward scenery should not be ignored as the peat bogs from Loch Loyal eastward are regarded as being of world importance. This is the Flow Country, a wilderness relatively undisturbed by humans for at least 6000 or more years. It is home to such rarities as the freshwater pearl mussel, insectivorous plants such as the sundew and to birds – including 70 per cent of Europe's breeding population of greenshanks. Golden eagles, short-eared owls and peregrines all treat this as their hunting and breeding ground. Unfortunately, this beautiful and very desolate region is threatened by intensive forestry, often planted for tax advatanges rather that from a wish to grow a worthwhile crop, and a great debate is still continuing on how to preserve this fine example of Scotland's natural heritage for future generations.

BACK TO NATURE

The variety of good habitats, the plentiful supply of fish and the low human population have encouraged huge numbers of seabirds to nest along the coast. Particular places of interest include Faraid Head (near Durness) for puffins; Duncansby Head for many different types of cliff-nesting seabirds; Dunnet Bay for sea duck, divers and gulls in winter; and Golspie for sea duck and in particular eider. Loch Fleet is home to many birds, especially waders, so keen birdwatchers may wish to make a detour off the A9 and follow the southern shore of the loch before returning to Dornoch

Dramatic Smoo Cave near Durness

responsible for 18 deaths. It is said that he was so worried that his remains would be dug up after burial by families seeking revenge, he offered a local landowner a huge sum of money to reserve this tomb where he thought his bones might be safe. In many ways, the Balnakeil Craft Village is a memorial to days gone by. It was planned by the Ministry of Defence as an 'early warning station' but by the time it was built the technology was obsolete so the buildings were abandoned. They were subsequently taken up by craftsmen and women and their families who together have built up one of the Highlands' most fascinating communities. Crafts such as marquetry, knitting, pottery and woodturning are represented here and each of the craft shops has a display where the high-quality goods can be viewed.

Cape Wrath is reached by ferry and bus from the Kyle of Durness. The headland at Cape Wrath, the northwestern tip of mainland Britain, rises 360 feet (110m) from the sea and is topped by a lighthouse built by the grandfather of Robert Louis Stevenson, in 1828. The area between the cape and the kyle is a vast expanse of peat bog known as the Parph and comes to an abrupt end at the coast which has the highest cliffs on the mainland, the biggest being Clo Mor, which is over 600 feet (180m) high.

A potter at work at Balnakeil Crafts Village

i *Sango, Durness (seasonal)*

▶ *Return along the A838 to Tongue, then follow the A836 along the coast to Bettyhill.*

4 **Bettyhill,** Highland
Bettyhill was founded by people displaced during the Clearances and the name derives from Elizabeth, Countess of Sutherland, wife of the duke who was responsible for many of the region's evictions. The local Strathnaver Museum is housed in a church built in 1774 and in the churchyard stands the Farr Stone, a good example of early Christian Celtic sculpture. The museum has features on the local

clearances as Strathnaver was one of the centres of the evictions. To the south of Bettyhill stand the remains of the clearance village of Achanlochy, where seven families were thrown out of their homes.

The village stands close to the River Naver and looks over sandy Torrisdale Bay, on the southern side of which is the Invernaver Nature Reserve. Its flora is of an unusual mix as blown shell-sand has mixed with the otherwise acid soil and supports a wide variety of plants, including dwarf juniper, thrift, alpine bistort and creeping willow.

i   *Clachan, Bettyhill (seasonal)*

▶ *Continue on the A836 to Reay.*

5   **Reay,** Highland
The original Reay was buried in sand in the early 18th century, but the village was rebuilt and the local church dates from 1839 when the new community was being re-established. Reay has given its name to the 'Reay Country', the great inland tract of deer 'forest', though it should be noted that when the word

'forest' is used to describe a hunting ground, it does not necessarily imply that there are many trees there!

Today, Reay is best known for the hemispherical dome of the nearby nuclear reactor at Dounreay. In 1955 construction of the Dounreay Fast Reactor was begun in order to produce electricity. In 1974 the Prototype Fast Reactor began operating. Neither of these plants now produce electricity, but the site does have a visitor centre.

▶ *Continue on the A836 for 12 miles (19km) to Thurso.*

6   **Thurso,** Highland
Thurso began life as a fishing settlement and the fishermen's houses can be seen above the harbour. However, it developed rapidly in the early 19th century when huge quantities of Caithness 'flags' were exported. These are the flat slabs of local sandstone that were in demand for pavements in the greatly expanding towns and cities of Britain and other countries. The flags are so common that even local fences are made of them.

Today, Thurso has again

The ruins of Old St Peters' Kirk in Thurso

expanded dramatically as a result of the building of the reactors at Dounreay. However, it still has a number of substantial sandstone buildings and these help to retain its homely character. The 17th-century Thurso Castle overlooks the harbour and beyond it Harold's Tower, erected over the grave of Earl Harold, the 12th-century ruler whose domain covered parts of Caithness, Orkney and Shetland.

The Thurso Heritage Museum contains a wide variety of interesting artefacts, including the Ulbster Stone (a Pictish sculptured stone), and also an important collection of rocks and fossils collected by Robert Dick in the 19th century.

Northwest of Thurso, on the A836, is the village of Mey. The Castle of Mey is the summer residence of the Queen Mother.

i   *Riverside (seasonal)*

▶ *Continue on the A836 for 20 miles (32km) to John o' Groats.*

7 John o' Groats, Highland
This is often thought to be mainland Britain's most northerly point, but in fact Dunnet Head (to the west) holds that distinction. However, it is the country's most northerly village and therefore either the start or finish of the ever popular John o' Groats to Land's End long-distance walks. The village was named after Jan de Groot, a Dutchman who started a ferry service from here to Orkney in the 16th century.

Near by, Duncansby Head, the northeastern tip of the mainland, has cliffs 210 feet (64m) high and a lighthouse. With care, the cliff tops can be followed to view the pinnacles called the Stacks of Duncansby and other sea stacks and cliffs that the sea has carved out of the sandstone.

further north, the 15th-century Castle Girnigoe and 17th-century Castle Sinclair remain, though reduced to spectacular clifftop ruins.

Wick is still an important and busy place, with a fine harbour that was originally built for the once-prosperous herring industry. An earlier harbour was built at Pulteneytown by Thomas Telford in 1806 to encourage evicted crofters to take up fishing. Wick's Heritage Centre, on Bank Row, is in the heart of a district of old buildings associated with the fishing industry, and has displays on the history of the town and the herring industry. On High Street stands Wick's old parish church, with the ruined 13th-century chapel of St Fergus in its grounds.

The Last House in John O'Groats, erroneously thought to be Britain's most northerly point

i County Road (seasonal)

▶ Leave by the **A99** to Wick.

8 Wick, Highland
Wick has been an important anchorage at least since the days of the Vikings; its name means 'bay'. Three castles testify to its strategic importance. The 12th-century castle of Old Wick stands to the south of the town;

i Whitechapel Road, off High Street

▶ Remain on the **A99**. Turn right at a signposted unclassified road to the Hill o' Many Stones.

9 Hill o' Many Stones, Highland
This intriguing fan-shaped array of 22 rows of stones dates back to the early Bronze Age, and is a type of monument unique to northern Sutherland (though they are similar to ones found in Brittany). Their purpose is still an unravelled mystery though it has been said that this could be some sort of ancient computer used to predict the movement of heavenly bodies.

FOR HISTORY BUFFS

Pictish brochs can be found in many places on this tour. The most substantial ones near the route are Cairn Laith (south of Brae) and Ousdale Broch (north of Helmsdale). Good ones further off the route are Dun Dornaigil (south of Loch Hope) and Grummore Broch (north of Loch Naver).

▶ Continue on the **A99** and **A9** for 13 miles (21km) to Dunbeath.

10 Dunbeath, Highland
Dunbeath was the home of Highland writer Neil Gunn, whose books include *The Silver Darlings*. The local Heritage Centre (housed in the school that Gunn attended) has displays on the lives of crofters and the history of the district. Laidhay Croft Museum, just north of the village, occupies a traditional longhouse and barn steading worked up until 1968. Parts of this thatched building may date back to the late 18th century though most of it is mid-19th-century.

▶ Continue on the **A9** for 16 miles (26km) to Helmsdale.

SPECIAL TO . . .

With the fishing industry and farming facing economic problems, new skills are being learned by the local people. The craftspeople of Caithness Glass (on the outskirts of Wick) come into this category, although their level of production is much greater than the average small-scale craft workshop. The factory has a visitor centre and tours are available.

11 Helmsdale, Highland
Set on the River Helmsdale, at the seaward end of the attractive Strath of Kildonan, this was where some of the most infamous acts of the Clearances were carried out by Patrick Sellars on behalf of the Countess of Sutherland. The story of these sad days is admirably told in Helmsdale's Timespan Heritage Centre. This award-winning exhibition also has an exhibition on the Kildonan 'gold rush' of 1868–69. Although gold was never found in economically viable quantities, some people still go panning in the river and find small flakes of the metal.

i *Cooper Park (seasonal)*

▶ *Continue on the A9 to Brora.*

12 Brora, Highland
Brora has the unusual distinction of having had a small coal mine based on a seam 'only' 125 million years old and, of course, a great distance from the country's main coalfields in the Midland Valley.

Today, one of its most notable industries is the Clynelish Distillery, Sutherland's only malt whisky distillery; tours are available.

▶ *Continue on the A9 to Golspie.*

13 Golspie, Highland
This small resort lies beneath the wooded slope of Beinn a' Bhragaidh, near whose summit is perched a statue of the first Duke of Sutherland, who was known as the 'Leviathan of Wealth'. Between the years 1810 and 1820 he was responsible for the eviction of some 15,000 tenants from their homes, in order to use the land for lucrative sheep farming. The scars of these times are still visible all over Sutherland. Ruined croft buildings stand and decay where families were forcibly moved from their land. A rather unusual shop in the village is the Orcadian Stone Company,

which sells examples of rocks, minerals and fossils. It also has a fine exhibition of these natural treasures.

The Dukes of Sutherland built nearby Dunrobin Castle on a site that has been fortified for many centuries. The present castle dates mainly from the 13th century but much of it was built between 1835 and 1850. Queen Victoria described it as a 'mixture of an old Scotch castle and a French château' and it does have a certain fairy-tale look about it. The gardens are extensive and contain a museum with interesting Pictish stones, an ice-house (for storing perishable food) and an 18th-century doocot.

South of Golspie, the main road crosses the head of Loch Fleet, over a huge earthen embankment known as The Mound. This was constructed in 1816 by Thomas Telford, partly to support the new road heading northwards, but also to reclaim the upper reaches of the loch. Today, this section is colonised by alder and willow

Above: Panning for gold in the Kildonan Burn, Helmsdale. Right: The fairytale Dunrobin Castle, one of Queen Victoria's favourite places

and has been classed as a National Nature Reserve. The River Fleet runs through a sluice at the end of the embankment and at certain times of the year salmon may be seen there waiting for the gate to open so they can continue their journey.

▶ *Continue on the A9, then turn left at the B9168 in order to return to Dornoch, 11 miles (17km).*

SCENIC ROUTES

The superb coastal scenery, both cliffs and beaches, make this tour very attractive, especially along the north coast and near the high headlands in the northeast. The Strath of Kildonan is a fine drive for those wishing a detour.

Easter Ross &
the Black Isle

Away from the dramatic Highlands scenery of previous chapters, this tour takes in gentler countryside and coastal roads. The tour begins in Dingwall, a town which has enjoyed a chequered history, having been a Viking settlement and later a market town with the status of a royal burgh.

2 DAYS • 173KM • 107 MILES

ITINERARY		
DINGWALL	▶	**Evanton (6m-10km)**
EVANTON	▶	**Tain (21m-34km)**
TAIN	▶	**Portmahomack**
		(10m-16km)
PORTMAHOMACK	▶	**Fearn Abbey (7m-11km)**
FEARN ABBEY	▶	**Cromarty (37m-60km)**
CROMARTY	▶	**Rosemarkie (9m-14km)**
ROSEMARKIE	▶	**Fortrose (1m-2km)**
FORTROSE	▶	**Dingwall (16m-26km)**

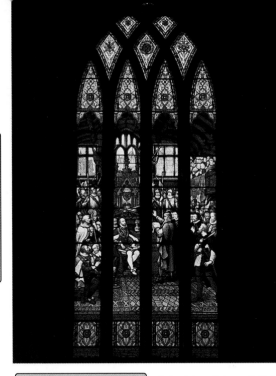

Stained glass window at St Duthus' church, Tain

▶ *Leave by the **A862**. Join the **A9** heading northwards, then turn left at the **B817** to Evanton.*

SCENIC ROUTES

The sea views are particularly striking especially when driving past the firths' narrowest parts. One of the best known views is found on the Struie road; as this road descends there is a viewpoint on the right overlooking the Kyle of Sutherland.

❶ Evanton, Highland

From the road, a curious monument will be seen on the summit of Cnoc Fyrish, the hill just beyond Evanton. This is a folly built in 1782 by General Sir Hector Munro to help alleviate local unemployment. The general had served in India and this monument is a replica of an Indian gate.

To the north of the village, the River Glass runs through a narrow glen, the narrowest part of which is known as the Black Rock Gorge. This intriguing cleft is 200 feet (60m) deep in some parts and only 10 feet (3m) wide. A narrow bridge over a 70-foot (20m) drop can be walked over by visitors.

▶ *Continue on the **B817** and turn left at the **B9176** (the Struie road). Turn right at the **A836** and join the **A9** for Tain. Bear left after 2 miles (3km) to enter Tain.*

❷ Tain, Highland

Tain's name comes from the Norse word 'thing', meaning a parliament, as a Viking colony was established in this district. Later, the town's patron, St Duthus, was born here (in AD1000) and he established a chapel just outside the town. He died in Ireland, but his remains were brought back and interred in the 14th-century St Duthus' Church. The town subsequently became a place of pilgrimage and James IV often travelled here, thus increasing its prestige and importance.

Tain's history was blotted, however, when it became an administrative centre for the Clearances. It was here that orders for the appropriation of the crofters' land were made. The deeds were carried out from the Tolbooth that still stands in the High Street, and it was within this building that crofters were imprisoned if they refused to obey the eviction notices. The Tolbooth is Tain's finest building; it was built between 1706 and 1733 with fine conical roofs on top of the turrets, and replaced an earlier tolbooth of 1631.

At Castle Brae, the Tain Through Time exhibition describes the history of the town; the centre also includes St Duthus' Church.

The Glenmorangie Distillery, renowned for its single malt whisky, lies on the outskirts of town.

RECOMMENDED WALKS

The walk at Evanton to see the Black Rock Gorge is worthwhile, as is the nervewracking walk over the narrow bridge at the gorge. Walks to lighthouses or looking points are usually interesting: try Tarbat Ness (a circular walk from Portmahomack via the coastal path that goes past Ballone Castle) or the lookout at the top of the Sutors of Cromarty.

Publicans' copper measures, Tain Museum

The fishing village of Portmahomack

▶ Leave by the minor road to Portmahomack. Turn left at the **B9165** to enter the village.

❸ Portmahomack, Highland

This pleasant lobster-fishing village sits in a broad bay with views across the Dornoch Firth. Just by the main street, an ornate Victorian cast-iron fountain celebrates the introduction of 'gravitation water' to the village in 1887 (water had previously come up from a well). Another unusual structure is the tower of the local church which is domed.

Beyond the village, a minor road leads to a lighthouse at Tarbat Ness. To the east of Portmahomack stand the ruins of Ballone Castle which can be reached from either the village or the lighthouse.

▶ Return along the **B9165** for 7 miles (11km) to Fearn Abbey

❹ Fearn Abbey, Highland

The original abbey was founded in the 13th century and is unfortunately best known for the collapse of its roof in 1742, which killed 42 people. This had been prophesied by the Brahan Seer, Coinneach Odhar. The 16th-

---

BACK TO NATURE

Both the Dornoch and the Cromarty Firth are good for birdwatching, particularly for waders when the tide is out. Since the district projects some distance into the North Sea it is the first landfall for many migratory birds and Tarbat Ness is often a temporary resting place for visiting birds on their migratory routes. The best times of year are April and May and August and October, particularly when the winds are from the east.

---

century clairvoyant had the gift of the 'second sight' and during his life he gave many warnings of unhappy events that were to happen. Many of these came true and his penultimate prophecy, telling of the infidelity of the Countess of Seaforth's husband, led to him being burned alive in a barrel of tar. His last prophecy, made just before he died, foretold of the extinction of the Seaforth family. That took place in the early 19th century. Brahan, where he came from, is an estate to the south-west of Dingwall.

FOR HISTORY BUFFS

The great Pictish cross slab, known as Clach a'Charridh, stands above the seaside village of Shandwick, near Balintore. It stands in its original position, and the face looking out to sea is engraved with a cross, angels and a beast. The other side has fivel panels, one of which shows a Pictish beast.

▶ Continue on the **B9165** and turn left at the **A9**. Cross the Cromarty Firth, then turn left at the **B9163** to Cromarty.

❺ Cromarty, Highland

Cromarty stands at the entrance to the Cromarty Firth, a passage dominated by the headlands of the Sutors of Cromarty and the North Sutor on the opposite shore. This is an important anchorage and was used during both world wars. Today, the firth has an oil rig fabrication site and these massive rigs dominate the sheltered waters.

The village was once important as it was on the main route north from Inverness which ran along the coast and used a series of ferries across the various stretches of water. The village declined after the fishing failed and after it was decided that the railway route was to go on the other side of the firth. The most outstanding building from more prosperous times is the Town House, built in the 18th century. This contains the courthouse and has been opened as a visitor centre.

Cromarty's most notable inhabitant was Hugh Miller, whose cottage has been preserved by the National Trust for Scotland. Miller was a stonemason by trade but he never lost his childhood curiosity for collecting fossils and interesting rocks. He helped to popularise geology as he avoided the jargon of the professionals and he wrote a widely read series of articles entitled *The Old Red Sandstone*, published in 1841. However, Miller had strong religious ideas that contradicted his scientific findings and his writings were furiously attacked by the religious bigots of the day. His thatched cottage, built in the early 18th century, contains mementoes of his life. Within the house is an example of the fossil fish named after him, *Pterichthys milleri*, and outside stands a sundial that he carved himself.

▶ *Leave by the A832 and follow it to Rosemarkie.*

❻ Rosemarkie, Highland

With red sandstone houses and a red sandy beach to match, attractive Rosemarkie sits at the mouth of the Moray Firth opposite Fort George. St Moluag founded a monastic school here in the 6th century and a Pictish stone in the local churchyard is said to mark the saint's resting place. Other carved stones are amongst

The remains of Fortrose's medieval cathedral

the exhibits in the local museum in Groam House, which has special displays on the Picts and the Brahan Seer. The Fairy Glen, reputedly the home of a witch, runs inland from the village and there are two waterfalls further up this nicely wooded valley.

▶ *Continue on the A832 for 1 mile (2km) to Fortrose.*

❼ Fortrose, Highland

Fortrose's main attraction is its medieval cathedral, which has an octagonal clock tower and a detached Chapter House. The local bishopric was originally at Rosemarkie, but it moved to Fortrose in the early years of the 13th century and work on the new cathedral was started at that time,

although it was not completed until the 15th century. A treasure trove of over 1,000 medieval coins was discovered buried in the green in 1880.

The harbour is well-sheltered but is now mainly used by pleasure craft. From the village, a narrow neck of land stretches out into the Moray Firth to Chanonry Point where there is a lighthouse. It was here that the Brahan Seer was burned to death, and a monument has been set up to celebrate this rather remarkabl man.

▶ *Continue on the A832 to the Tore roundabout join the A835 and turn right at the A862 to return to Dingwall.*

Fortrose cathedral: detail

Over the Sea
to Skye

Skye is the most scenically spectacular island of the whole of the British Isles, with glorious mountain landscapes. The gateway to Skye, Kyleakin, is guarded by the ruin of Castle Moil, a small Norse keep. The village is crowded during the summer months as this is the terminus of the railway line from Inverness.

2/3 DAYS • 392KM • 244 MILES

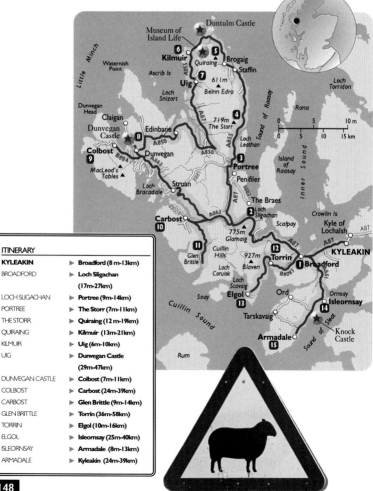

▶ Leave by the **A850** and follow it for 8 miles (13km) to Broadford.

1 Broadford, Highland
This widely scattered crofting community lies beneath the Red Hills, a group of rounded granite mountains. This is a good base from which to explore the south of the island and is popular with walkers and other visitors.

▶ Continue on the **A87** to the Sligachan Hotel at the head of Loch Sligachan.

2 Loch Sligachan, Highland
This is an idyllic base for any visitor, and especially for those who come to walk in the Cuillin Hills. The campsite by the shore must surely rate as one of Britain's finest, not for its facilities but for its position by the lochshore opposite towering 2,544-foot (775m) Glamaig, and the view across the Inner Sound towards the mainland. A stroll from the road leads to an old bridge over the River Sligachan from which the Cuillin Hills can be seen to greater advantage.

The Cuillin Hills, reflected in the waters of Loch Sligachan

▶ Continue on the **A87** for 9 miles (14km) to Portree.

3 Portree, Highland
This is the island's 'capital' and although the islanders themselves might think of it as a busy place, the pace of life follows the generally relaxed Highland pattern. This is certainly a most picturesquely positioned town, with its well-sheltered harbour nestling at the foot of wooded hills.
The town's name, Port an Righ, or 'king's port', celebrates the visit here in 1540 by James V in his attempt to persuade local chiefs that they should swear allegiance to him. He brought 12 ships with him to help them make up their minds!

ⅰ Meall House (Portree)

▶ Leave by the **A855** and continue for 7 miles (11km) to The Storr (after Loch Leathan).

FOR HISTORY BUFFS

South of Portree, the B883 road leads to the settlement of Braes, where a monument celebrates the battles between local crofters and the police in 1882. The locals had asked their Laird, Lord MacDonald, for extra land on which to graze their animals. He refused, even though the crofters were prepared to pay, and they decided to withhold their rents. Court orders were then taken out against them but the orders were siezed and torn up when the sheriff's officers tried to deliver them.
In a further confrontation, the local police were helped by 50 policemen from Glasgow (and backed up by naval ships standing by with troops aboard should the 'trouble' spread). These events caused a public outcry about the way in which landowners treated crofters and this led to legislation being passed which guaranteed fair rents and security of tenure.

4 The Storr, Highland

As the road heads northwards it runs beneath a steep escarpment, the highest point of which is The Storr, 2,363 feet (719m) high. To the right of this can be seen the tall pinnacle called the Old Man of Storr which is 160 feet (49m) tall. This is the site of Britain's most spectacular example of landslipping; the jumble of boulders, screes and pinnacles indicates where chunks of the mountain have slipped as the weak underlying clays and limestones collapsed under the weight of the overlying lavas.

SCENIC ROUTES

In good weather the whole of this tour passes through scenery which is truely memorable. Perhaps the most dramatic parts are north of Portree when the Old Man of Storr is seen with Loch Fada in the foreground, and also going down Glen Brittle and seeing the massive northern corries of the Cuillin Hills.

▶ *Continue on the **A855** for 12 miles (19km) to the Quiraing.*

5 Quiraing, Highland

To the northwest of the crofting community of Staffin, another escarpment indicates the site of a massive landslip. This is known as the Quiraing and is best approached on foot from the Staffin to Uig road. Nature has produced some strange shapes here, and some of the features have been given names like the Table, the Prison and the Needle.

▶ *Continue on the **A855** for 13 miles (21km) to Kilmuir.*

6 Kilmuir, Highland

This scattered crofting community is home to the Skye Museum of Island Life which has a number of attractive thatched cottages that have been restored to show how people lived in these small houses a century ago. Near by, a tall monument in the local graveyard marks the grave of Flora MacDonald. She has a very special place in Scottish history as the woman who helped Bonnie Prince Charlie escape after Culloden. He had fled to South Uist but found the island crawling with hundreds of government soldiers, all of them keen to capture a man with a price of £30,000 on his head. Flora disguised the Prince as her maidservant Betty Burke and smuggled him over to Skye, from where he was able to reach the mainland and make his escape to safety in France.

To the north of Kilmuir stand the ruins of Duntulm Castle, built in the early 17th century by the Mac-Donalds. The building stands on a crag, protected by cliffs and steep slopes on the three seaward sides and a dry ditch on the landward side.

▶ *Continue on the **A855** to Uig.*

The Old Man of Storr on the Isle of Skye

Flora MacDonald's grave at Kilmuir

7 Uig, Highland
This little port is the terminus for the ferries that serve Lochmaddy on North Uist and Tarbert on Harris, so the harbourside can be busy around sailing times. A little tower overlooks the harbour and though it looks rather old, it is in fact a Victorian folly dating back to the 19th century.

▶ *Leave by the A87 and turn right when the A850 is met. Follow this to Dunvegan Castle.*

8 Dunvegan Castle, Highland
The home of the chiefs of Clan MacLeod was built as a keep in the 14th century with its only entrance through the sea gate. Within the castle is the famous 'fairy flag', said to have been given to a MacLeod chief by his fairy wife. The flag is of Eastern origin and according to the legend it will protect the clan if waved at moments of great danger. Also on display is the drinking horn owned by the chieftain Sir Rory Mor: this can

hold the equivalent of two bottles of wine, and it is claimed that he could drain it in one draught!

On the other side of Loch Dunvegan stand the two flat-topped hills called MacLeod's Tables. Their name recalls a chieftain bragging to a Lowlander of the size of his dining table; to prove his boast

View of the ferry loading at Uig

he entertained his guest on one of the summits.

▶ *Leave by the A863, then turn right at the B884 to Colbost.*

9 Colbost, Highland

There is a little folk museum here with a thatched cottage and a display of 19th-century furniture and farming implements. If you have never smelled a peat fire burning then here is your chance!

▶ *Return along the B884 and turn right at the A863. Turn right at the B8009 and follow this to Carbost.*

FOR CHILDREN

The moors and lower hills of Skye provide good terrain for pony trekking and there are facilities at Struan (south of Dunvegan on the A832), Penifiler (south of Portree) and Uig. However, it must be remembered that Skye's weather can be very mixed.

---

10 Carbost, Highland

This is the site of Skye's only distillery, the Talisker Distillery. The peat fires used to dry the grain gives the whisky its distinctive smokey flavour.

▶ *Return along the B8009 and turn right at the minor road that leads down Glen Brittle.*

11 Glen Brittle, Highland

Most visitors to Skye will have heard of the Cuillin Hills, the serrated ridges of which provide marvellous hillwalking. Many of the hills' lower slopes are covered with loose scree, while many of the upper parts are bare rock with little or no vegetation on them, and these are the preserve of experienced hillwalkers. For walkers trying to capture all the 'Munros' (Scottish hills with a peak over 3,000 feet [914m] high), their most difficult obstacle is usually the Inaccessible Pinnacle on Sgurr Dearg which involves climbing a pinnacle at the top of the mountain. Definitely not for casual walkers, who would be best advised to stick to easier walks in the area.

The foot of the glen is often busy with walkers and climbers who are here to scale the hills. Looking up and around, there are marvellous views of the jagged hills with their long steep scree slopes.

▶ *Return to the B8009 and turn right. Turn right at the A863 and continue to Sligachan, then turn right at the A87. Follow this to Broadford, then turn right at the B8083 in order to reach Torrin.*

The Cuillin Hills seen above Loch Scavaig, near Elgol

12 Torrin, Highland

Torrin is best known for its fine view of the 3,044-foot (928m) mountain, Blà Bheinn (or Blaven) and its precipitous rocky ridge known as Clach Glas. The latter entices the experienced climber. A couple of quarries near by are sources of the white Skye marble.

▶ *Continue on the B8083 and follow it to Elgol.*

13 Elgol, Highland

Elgol, overlooking Loch Scavaig, has a small jetty from which there is one of the best views of the Cuillin Hills. From here it is possible to appreciate the shape of the complex, with a ring of hills surrounding Loch Coruisk. Boat trips to Loch Coruisk are available from Elgol. Looking in the other direction, the breathtaking view over the sea encompasses the islands of Soay, Rum, Canna and Eigg.

▶ *Return along the B8083 as far as Broadford, then turn right at the A87. Turn right again at the A851 to Isleornsay.*

14 Isleornsay, Highland
The village lies a little off the main road. At the road end is a headland on which there is an inn, a pier and a view towards the tidal island of Ornsay. The wilderness of Knoydart stands opposite, on the other side of the Sound of Sleat. Further

south lies Knock Bay and above this is a rocky mound on which stands Knock Castle. These ivy-covered ruins are sometimes called Castle Camus. It was built in medieval times by the MacDonalds of Sleat and its best known occupant was a lady known as Mary of the Castle.

▶ *Continue on the **A851** for 8 miles (13km) to Armadale.*

15 Armadale, Highland
Armadale can be a busy little place at times as it has a car ferry connection with Mallaig, but it is really a very picturesque spot in a sheltered bay. Close to the village stands the Clan Donald Visitor Centre. This is in the grounds of the now partly ruined Armadale Castle, which was built in 1815, and has interesting displays on the history of the MacDonalds. There are also gardens and woodland trails in the grounds. This part of Skye,

known as Sleat, is sometimes called the 'Garden of Skye' because of its luxuriant coastal vegetation. Dr Johnson visited Armadale in 1773 and was duly impressed by what he saw of the fine gardens here, commenting that the planting of the gardens 'proved that the present nakedness of the Hebrides is not wholly the fault of Nature'. An alternative route back to Isleornsay (instead of taking the A851) is via Tarskavaig on the western side of Sleat. This route gives really superb views over to Soay and Rum. There are also fine unspoiled beaches at Tarskavaig Bay and Ord.

▶ *Return along the **A851** towards Broadford. Turn right at the **A87** to return to Kyleakin.*

Isolated church and graveyard on the road to Elgol

Spanish Gold &
Celtic Crosses

Mull is an island of great beauty and emptiness. Its capital,
Tobermory, can be a busy place in the summer, with Main Street
thronged with cars, caravans and visitors, while its bay is usually
full of pleasure boats. In 1588 a galleon of the Spanish Armada
sank in the bay, and rumours of sunken gold still abound.

1/2 DAYS • 231KM • 143 MILES

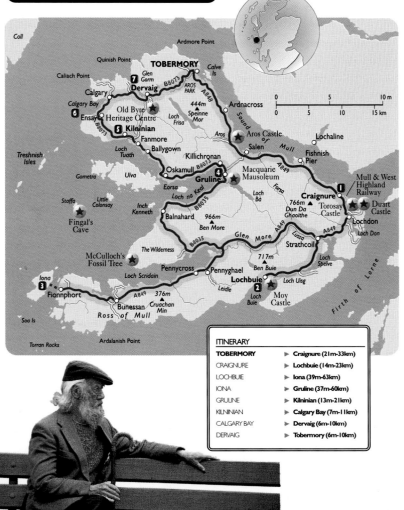

ITINERARY		
TOBERMORY	►	**Craignure (21m-33km)**
CRAIGNURE	►	**Lochbuie (14m-23km)**
LOCHBUIE	►	**Iona (39m-63km)**
IONA	►	**Gruline (37m-60km)**
GRULINE	►	**Kilninian (13m-21km)**
KILNINIAN	►	**Calgary Bay (7m-11km)**
CALGARY BAY	►	**Dervaig (6m-10km)**
DERVAIG	►	**Tobermory (6m-10km)**

FOR HISTORY BUFFS

Just north of Salen stands the ruined tower of Aros Castle. Like Duart Castle further down the coast, this commands a fine view over the Sound of Mull and was an important bastion of the powerful Lords of the Isles, the rulers of this region of Scotland from the 14th to the 16th centuries.

Torosay Castle gardens: statue details

i *Main Street*

▶ *Leave by the **A848** to Salen, then continue along the coast on the **A849** to Craignure.*

❶ Craignure, Strathclyde
This is the island's main ferry terminal and the first place in Mull that most visitors will see. Torosay Castle stands close to Craignure and visitors can reach it by driving further down the road, strolling along a forest walk from Craignure or taking a trip on the miniature railway. The castle is not a fortified structure, but a Victorian mansion built in 1856; it has extensive gardens designed by Sir Robert Lorimer and a 'statue garden' with 19 Italian figures.
A little further down the coast stands the strong-

View of the colourful harbour front, Tobermory

hold of Duart Castle. This was originally built in the 13th century by the MacDougalls but later passed into the hands of the Macleans. Much of the present structure comprises their 14th-century additions.

▶ *Follow the **A849** to Strathcoil, then turn left at the unclassified road to Lochbuie.*

❷ Lochbuie, Strathclyde
The minor road down to Lochbuie is narrow and winding and passes through a well-wooded glen and a landscape that is quite different from the open moorlands so common in much of Mull. At the shore, the wide bay is ringed by hills and to the east stands the ruined tower of Moy Castle, a Maclaine castle of the 15th century. This ivy-covered castle has a special dungeon off the dining room. It is a pit filled with water to a

Compared to many islands off the west coast, Mull has considerable areas of native woodland as well as plantations. Look for woodland birds here, while golden eagles and buzzards prefer rocky crags. Offshore, sea birds, including guillemots, can be seen while others feed unobtrusively along the shoreline.

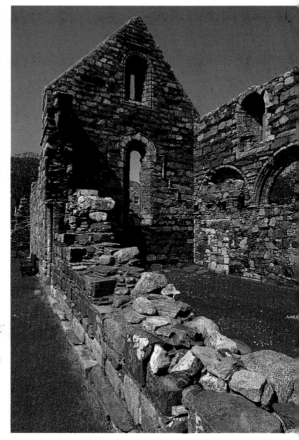

The ruined abbey on the Isle of Iona

depth of 9 feet (3m) with a stone sticking up in the middle of the pool; this is where the poor prisoner sat – in total darkness! The fertile land at the head of the loch earned the estate the name the 'Garden of Mull'. Behind Lochbuie House stands a reminder of a very early settlement, a stone circle with nine uprights and three outlying monoliths.

▶ *Return to the **A849** and turn left. Follow this road to Fionnphort and take the ferry over to Iona. Cars should be left at Fionnphort.*

❸ Iona, Strathclyde
The small island of Iona is a magnet for summer visitors, and is a place of great historic and spiritual significance. Part of Scotland's history is re-created in its abbey, now painstakingly reconstructed using traditional materials. The historic importance of Iona stems from the arrival here in AD563 of the Irish missionary Columba who established a monastery. The island became a religious centre and its influence spread throughout Scotland and into England, but it suffered at the hands of the Viking raiders in the 8th century. A Benedictine abbey was founded around the start of the 13th century and the oldest part of the abbey dates from that time. Until the time of the Reformation, there were over 300 crosses standing near the abbey but many were broken during those turbulent times and only a few massive examples now remain as beautifully carved memorials to the skills of the early craftsmen.

Apart from the abbey, there are a number of other buildings worth looking at, including the ruined Augustinian nunnery and St Oran's Chapel. The chapel is the oldest building on Iona. The story behinds its name involves its troubled construction. The walls kept collapsing and to placate the evil spirit that was felt to be causing this problem, it was decided that a human sacrifice was needed to be placed under the foundations – Oran was the volunteer. The chapel is in the Reilig Oran – the graveyard of kings – where many of Scotland's early kings and queens, and a number of Irish, Norwegian and possibly French kings are buried.

▶ *Return to Fionnphort and follow the **A849** eastwards. Turn left at the **B8035** to reach Gruline.*

❹ Gruline, Strathclyde
At Gruline, a narrow road (right) leads to the mausoleum of Major-General Lachlan Macquarie. Born locally, he followed a career in the British army before becoming Governor-General of New South Wales in Australia, a post he held from 1810 to 1820. In recognition of this connection, the building is maintained on behalf of the National Trust of Australia.

▶ Continue on the **B8035**, then turn left on to the **B8073** to reach Kilninian, 13 miles (21km).

▶ Continue on the **B8073** for 7 miles (11km) to Calgary Bay.

BACK TO NATURE

Much of Mull has been built up by basalt lavaflows from long-lost volcanoes and the island has some unique volcanic features that are worth seeing. The uninhabited peninsula on the northern side of Loch Scridain is aptly named 'The Wilderness' and on its southern shore is the world-famous McCulloch's Fossil Tree, a large conifer that was engulfed by lava. It can only be approached at low tide and then after a long walk, so careful preparation is needed for a visit.

6 Calgary Bay, Strathclyde
This wide bay with its sandy beach is a popular stopping place for visitors. Few people live here now, but on the northern side of the bay there are deserted townships and an old pier. The builders of the pier took full advantage of the local geology when they used a prominent volcanic dike as one of the walls. The existence of this prominent vertical sheet of rock could have led to the name of the bay, as Calgary may have come from the Gaelic word Calagharaidh, meaning 'the haven by the wall'. The town of Calgary in Alberta, Canada, was named after the bay.

▶ Continue on the **B8073** for 6 miles (10km) to Dervaig.

7 Dervaig, Strathclyde
Dervaig is a very pleasant little community that was established as a 'planned village' in 1799. The village and its environs have been designated a conservation area and this is a good base from which to explore the north of the island, Calgary and

FOR CHILDREN

There are a number of good beaches round the coast, notably at Calgary Bay, which is ideal for bathing, and Lochbuie. the narrow-guage railway at Torosay Castle is always appealing to children (and adults). This is the country's only island railway and was originally built in 1984 to encourage reluctant walkers to go from Craignure Pier to Torosay Castle; however, it has become an attraction in its own right. It has four engines, two of them steam-powered.

Tobermory. The most obvious village landmark is the church's round tower, reminiscent of Irish churches. The building is relatively modern, having been constructed as recently as 1905. Two other local places of interest are the Mull Little Theatre and, a little further out of the village, the Old Byre Heritage Centre, which depicts crofting life.

▶ Continue on the **B8073** and return to Tobermory.

5 Kilninian, Strathclyde
There has been a little church here overlooking the sea since at least 1561 but the present structure was built in 1755. At the back of the church there are a number of large carved grave slabs from the early 16th century. Dun Aisgain is found a little further along the road, standing on a rocky knoll overlooking the sea. This defensive site still has some of its 6-foot (2m) thick walls intact, and has traces of the internal mural gallery that was built within it. The Dun is best approached from Burg.

SCENIC ROUTES

Most of the coastal roads give fine views over the sea, especially the sections by Loch na Keal and Loch Tuath where there are excellent views of the offshore islands, the largest of which is Ulva, where the parents of Scots missionary, David Livingstone, came from.

The Isle of Mull's local steam railway

PRACTICAL INFORMATION

FACTS AND FIGURES

Bordered by: England.

IDD code: 44. To call an international number dial '00' followed by the country code, area code and finally number you require.

Currency: the unit of currency is the pound (£), divided into 100 pence. Coins are in denominations of 1, 2, 5, 10, 20 and 50 pence and one pound (£1); Scottish notes are in denominatons of £5, 10, 20 and 50. Bank of England notes are also legal tender.

Local time: the official time is Greenwich Mean Time (GMT). British Summer Time (BST) begins in late March when the clocks are put forward an hour. In late October, the clocks go back an hour to GMT. The official date of the changes is announced in the daily newspapers and is always at 2am on a Sunday.

Emergency services: Police, fire and ambulance tel: 999.

Business hours –
Banks: generally open 9am-3.30pm weekdays, through times do vary from bank to bank, with some closing for lunch. Many are open on Saturday mornings until noon. In more remote areas, times vary so it is advisable to check.
Shops: Monday to Saturday 8.30am–1.30pm, 3.30–7.30pm. Many closed Monday mornings and food shops often Thursday afternoons.
Post Offices: Post Offices generally open from 9–5.30, Monday to Friday and 9–noon on Saturday. Times and days may vary from place to place.

Credit and charge cards: these are widely accepted.

Tourist information:
Scottish Tourist Board, 23 Ravelston Terrace, Edinburgh, EH4 3EU. Tel: 0131 332 2433.

MOTORING IN SCOTLAND

ACCIDENTS
In the event of an accident, the vehicle should be moved off the carriageway wherever possible. If the vehicle is fitted with hazard warning lights, they should be used. If available, a red triangle should be placed on the road at least 165 feet (50m) before the obstruction and on the same side of the road.

If damage or injury is caused to any other person or vehicle you must stop, give your own and the vehicle owner's name and address and the registration number of the vehicle to anyone having reasonable grounds for requiring them. If you do not give your name and address at the time of the accident, report the accident to the police as soon as reasonably practicable, and in any case within 24 hours.

BREAKDOWNS
Visitors who bring their cars to Scotland and are members of a recognised automobile club may benefit from the services provided free of charge by the AA. Car rental companies normally provide cover with one or other of the major motoring organisations in Britain. On motorways there are emergency telephones at the side of the hard shoulder every mile (1.6km).

In the event of a breakdown, the vehicle should be moved off the carriageway wherever possible. If the vehicle is fitted with hazard warning lights, they should be used. If available, a red triangle should be placed on the road at least 165 feet (50m) before the obstruction and on the same side of the road.

CARAVANS
Brakes
Check that the caravan braking mechanism is correctly

adjusted. If it has a breakaway safety mechanism, the cable between the car and caravan must be firmly anchored so that the trailer brakes act immediately if the two part company.

Caravan and luggage trailers

Take a list of contents, especially if any valuable or unusual equipment is being carried, as this may be required on arrival in Britain. A towed vehicle should be readily identifiable by a plate in an accessible position showing the name of the make of the vehicle and the production and serial number.

Lights

Make sure that all the lights are working – rear lights, stop lights, numberplate lights, rear fog guard lamps and flashers (check that the flasher rate is correct: 60-120 times a minute).

Tyres

Both tyres on the caravan should be of the same size and type. Inspect them carefully: if you think they are likely to be more than three-quarters worn before you get back, replace them before you leave. If you notice uneven wear, scuffed treads, or damaged walls, get expert advice on whether the tyres are suitable for further use.

Find out the recommended tyre pressures from the caravan manufacturer.

CAR HIRE AND FLY/DRIVE

Drivers must hold, and have held for one year, a valid national licence or an International Driving Permit. The minimum age for hiring a car ranges from 18 to 25, depending on the model of car. With some companies, there is a maximum age limit of 70. You can arrange to pick up your car in one town and return it in another. If you are hirng a car, you can often get a good deal with a fly/drive package tour.

The larger car hire companies have desks at airports and branches in major towns. These may not be the cheapest; telephone around for the best deal.

CHILDREN

The following restrictions apply to children travelling in private motor vehicles:

Children under 3 years: front seat – appropriate child restraint must be worn; rear seats – appropriate child restraint must be worn if available.

Child aged 3 to 11 and under 1.5m tall: front seat – appropriate child restraint must be worn if available, if not, adult seat belt must be worn. Rear seat – appropriate child restraint must be worn if available, if not, adult seat belt must be worn if available.

Child aged 12 or 13 or younger child 1.5m or more in height – front and rear seats – adult seat belt must be worn if available.

Note: under no circumstances should a rear-facing restraint be used in a seat with an airbag.

CRASH (SAFETY) HELMETS

Visiting motorcyclists and their passengers must wear crash or safety helmets.

DOCUMENTS

You must have a valid driver's licence or an International Driving Permit. Holders of permits written in a foreign language are advised to obtain an official translation from an embassy or recognised automobile association. Non-EC nationals must have Green Card insurance.

DRINKING AND DRIVING

The laws regarding drinking and driving are strict and the penalties severe. The best advice is if you drink don't drive.

DRIVING CONDITIONS

Traffic drives on the left (it goes clockwise at roundabouts

[traffic circles], which crop up frequently at intersections). Speed-limit and destination signs use miles (one kilometre is roughly 5/8 of a mile). Motorways link most major cities; service areas are indicated well in advance.

Tolls are levied on certain bridges and tunnels. Roads in some areas of Scotland are very narrow. See also ROADS.

FUEL

Unleaded as well as leaded petrol and diesel is widely available, and an environmental petrol tax means that unleaded is always cheaper. Unleaded petrol has a minimum octane rating of 95, with super octane available from some stations with a rating of around 98. The most widely available leaded petrol is 'four-star', which has a minimum octane rating of 97. Petrol stations are usually self-service and tend to be situated in and around towns and on the motorways and major roads. Motorway service stations and some service stations on busy major roads and in large towns open round the clock, or at least late into the night. Most petrol stations accept credit cards.

INSURANCE

Fully comprehensive insurance, which covers you for some of the expenses incurred after a breakdown or an accident, is advisable.

LIGHTS

You must ensure your front and rear side lights and rear registration plate lights are lit at night. You must use headlights when visibility is seriously reduced and at night on all unlit roads and those where the street lights are more than 185m (600ft) apart.

ROADS

Roads in Scotland are generally good. In the Highlands and Islands of Scotland, however, and in some country areas the roads are often narrow. On single track roads pull into the passing places only if they are on your left, stop level with those on your right, the oncoming traffic will make the detour. Never hold up faster traffic approaching from behind; stop at suitable places to allow drivers to overtake. Try to travel outside the main rush hours of 8-9.30am and 4.30-6pm when visiting the larger cities and towns.

ROUTE DIRECTIONS
Throughout the book the following abbreviations are used for Scottish roads:
A – main roads
B – local roads
unclassified roads – minor roads (unnumbered)

SEAT BELTS
Seat belts are compulsory for drivers and front seat passenger. Passengers travelling in the rear of the vehicle must wear a seat belt if fitted.

SPEED LIMITS
Speed limits for cars are 70mph (112kph) for motorways and dual carriageways, 60mph (96kph) for other roads, and 30mph (48kph) in built-up areas unless otherwise indicated.

TOLLS
Tolls are levied on certain bridges and tunnels.

WARNING TRIANGLE/HAZARD WARNING LIGHTS
If the vehicle is fitted with hazard warning lights, they should be used in the event of a breakdown or accident. If available, a red triangle should be placed on the road at least 165 feet (50m) before the obstruction and on the same side of the road.

CAMPING AND CARAVANNING SITES
There are many camp sites in Scotland, ranging from small fields with just a single cold tap by way of facilities to large-scale sites with shower blocks and

shops, but it should be remembered that many areas are isolated and have few sites and therefore it is necessary to plan in advance. A useful source of information is the list published by the Camping and Caravanning Club, East Grinstead House, East Grinstead, West Sussex, RH19 1UA. Tel: 01203 694995. Tourist Information Centres can also help by providing lists of local sites.

Off-site camping
If you are thinking of camping in the wilds, be aware of all that the Scottish climate can throw at you, and remember that even open moorland is owned by someone – try to ask permission first if possible. Off-site camping is discouraged on several of the Scottish Islands – check first.

Wherever possible the sites listed are on the tour route, but due to the shortage of sites in isolated areas, the sites shown marked with an asterisk are within a reasonable distance of the tour, but not actually on the route. Booking is advisable at most sites on Bank Holidays and during high season.

TOUR I
AYR South Ayrshire
Heads of Ayr Leisure Park
Dunure Road KA7 4LD (tel: 01292 442269)
5 miles south of Ayr off A719.
Open March to November.

MAYBOLE South Ayrshire
The Ranch Culzean Road KA19 8DU (tel: 01655 882446)
1 mile south of Maybole towards Culzean off B7023.
Open March to October and weekends in winter, except Christmas. Phone to check.

*COYLTON South Ayrshire
Sundrum Castle Holiday Park KA6 6HX (tel: 01292 570057)
Turn right from A77 on to A70, 3 miles east of Ayr.
Open March to October.

*TARBOLTON
South Ayrshire
Middlemuir Park KA5 5NR (tel: 01292 541647)
Turn right off B743 – signposted.
Open all year.

TOUR 2
NEWTON STEWART
Dumfries & Galloway
Creebridge Caravan Park
Minnigaff DG8 6AJ (tel: 01671 402324 and 402432)
2 miles east of Newton Stewart on bypass A75.
Open April to October.

Talnotry Campsite Queens Way DG8 7BL (tel: 01671 402420)
7 miles northeast of Newton Stewart off A712 – signposted.
Open April to September.

GLENLUCE
Dumfries & Galloway
Glenluce Caravan and Camping Park DG8 0QR (tel: 01581 300412)
Close to village centre off the A75.
Open March to October.

SANDHEAD
Dumfries & Galloway
Sands of Luce Caravan Park
DG9 9JR (tel: 01776 830456)
Turn off A75 on to the B7084.
Site is on the left after about 5 miles.
Open mid March to October.

PORTPATRICK
Dumfries & Galloway
Galloway Point Holiday Park
Portree Farm DG9 9AA (tel: 01776 810561)
1 mile south of town.
Open March to October.

STRANRAER
Dumfries & Galloway
Aird Donald Caravan Park
London Road DG9 8RN (tel: 01776 702025)
On edge of town.
Open all year.

CAIRNRYAN
Dumfries & Galloway
Cairnryan Caravan & Chalet

Park DG9 8QX (tel: 01581 200231)
Open Easter to October.

BARRHILL
South Ayrshire
Windsor Holiday Park KA26 0PZ (tel: 01465 821355)
1 mile northwest of village off A714.
Open all year.

TOUR 3
*SOUTHERNESS
Dumfries & Galloway
Southerness Holiday Village DG2 8AZ (tel: 01387 880256 and 880281)
Turn left off A710, site near centre of village.
Open March to October.

SANDYHILLS
Dumfries & Galloway
Sandyhills Bay Leisure Park DG5 4NY (tel: 01557 870267 and 01387 780257)
Open April to October.

DALBEATTIE
Dumfries & Galloway
Islecroft Caravan & Camping Site Colliston Park, Mill St DG5 4HE (tel: 01556 610012 and 01557 330291 ext 323)
On edge of town, close to local park.
Open Easter to September.

KIRKCUDBRIGHT
Dumfries & Galloway
Seaward Caravan Park Dhoon Bay DG6 4TJ (tel: 01557 870267 and 331079)
Off B727 Borgue Road.
Open March to October.

Silvercraigs Caravan & Camping Site Silvercraigs Road DG6 4BT (tel: 01557 330123 and 330291)
Close to town centre.
Open Easter to mid-October.
Phone for exact closing date.

GATEHOUSE OF FLEET
Dumfries & Galloway
Anwoth Caravan Site DG7 2JU (tel: 01557 814333)
Southwest of town.
Open 26 March to 1 October.

CREETOWN
Dumfries & Galloway
Castle Cary Holiday Park DG8 7DJ (tel: 01671 820264)
Open all year.

NEWTON STEWART
Dumfries & Galloway
Creebridge Caravan Park Minnigaff DG8 6AO (tel: 01671 402324 and 402432)
¼ mile east of Newton Stewart on bypass A75.
Open April to October.

Talnotry Campsite Queens Way DG8 7BL (tel: 01671 402420)
7 miles northeast of Newton Stewart off A712 – signposted.
Open April to September.

TOUR 4
*MOFFAT
Dumfries & Galloway
Camping & Caravanning Club Site Hammerlands Farm DG10 9QL (tel: 01683 220436 in season and 01203 694995)
Northeast of town off A708.
Open end March to early November.

BOTHWELL South Lanarkshire
Strathclyde Country Park Caravan Site Bothwellhaugh Road G71 8NY (tel: 01698 266155)
Close to junction 5 of M74.
Open April to October.

*KIRKFIELDBANK
South Lanarkshire
Clyde Valley Caravan Park ML11 9TS (tel: 01555 663951)
Just off A72 north of Lanark.
Open April to October.

TOUR 5
PEEBLES
Borders
Crossburn Caravan Park The Glades, 95 Edinburgh Road HE45 8ED (tel: 01721 720501)
Close to town.
Open April to October.

SELKIRK
Borders
Victoria Park Caravan &

Camping Park Victoria Park, Buccleuch Road TD7 5DN (tel: 01750 20897)
From A707/A708 north of town cross river bridge, take first left, then left again.
Site close to River Ettrick.
Open April to October.

MOFFAT
Dumfries & Galloway
Camping & Caravanning Club Site Hammerlands Farm DG10 9QL (tel: 01683 220436 in season and 01203 694995)
To the northeast of town off A708.
Open end March to early November.

TOUR 6
*KELSO Scottish Borders
Springwood Caravan Park TD5 8LS (tel: 01573 224596)
1 mile west of town off A698, south of Embleton on unclassified road.
Open end March to mid-October.

JEDBURGH Scottish Borders
Camping & Caravanning Club Site Elliot Park, Edinburgh Road TD8 6EF (tel: 01835 863393 in season and 01203 694995)
On northern edge of town, off A68.
Open end March to early November.

SELKIRK Borders
Victoria Park Caravan & Camping Park Victoria Park, Buccleuch Road TD7 5DN (tel: 01750 20897)
From A707/A708 north of town cross river bridge, take first left, then left again.
Picturesque site close to River Ettrick.
Open April to October.

TOUR 7
MUSSELBURGH
East Lothian
Drum Mohr Caravan Park Levenhall EH21 8JS (tel: 0131 665 6867)
2 miles east of town between A198 and B1348.
Open March to October.

DUNBAR East Lothian
Thurston Manor Holiday Home Park Innerwick EH42 1SA (tel: 01368 840643)
From A1, 6 miles north of Cockburnspath, take unclassified road signposted Innerwick, in 1/2 mile turn right, and site is 1/2 mile on right.
Open March to October.

COCKBURNSPATH
Borders
Chesterfield Caravan Site Neuk Farm TD13 5YH (tel: 01368 830459)
From A1 take unclassified road signposted Cockburnspath; the site is 5 miles along an unclassified road 200 yards south of village.
Open April to September.

*BERWICK-UPON-TWEED
Northumberland
Ord House Caravan Park East Ord TD15 2NS (tel: 01289 305288)
1 mile southwest of town on A698.
Open March to January.

KELSO
Borders
Springwood Caravan Park TD5 8LS (tel: 01573 224596)
1 mile west of town off A698, south of Embleton on unclassified road.
Open end March to October

LAUDER Borders
Thirlestane Castle Caravan & Camping Site Thirlestane Castle TD2 6RU (tel: 01578 722254)
In castle grounds off A697.
Open Easter to October.

DALKEITH Midlothian
Fordel Lauder Road EH22 2PH (tel: 0131 663 3046 & 0131 660 3921)
South of town on A68.
Open April to September.

EDINBURGH
City of Edinburgh
Mortonhall Caravan Park 38 Mortonhall Gate EH16 6TJ (tel: 0131 664 1533)

Located on south side of Edinburgh, within 20 minutes car ride of city centre, in the grounds of Mortonhall mansion. Follow A720 city bypass to junction with A702. Site signposted from here.
Open 28 March to October.

TOUR 8
OBAN Argyll & Bute
Oban Divers Caravan Park Glenshellach Road PA34 4QJ (tel: 01631 562755)
South of town.
Open 15 March to 15 November.

GLENCOE Highland
Invercoe Caravan Site PA39 4HP (tel: 01855 811210)
Edge of village, north of A82 on B863. On shore of Loch Leven.
Open Easter to mid-October.

INVERARAY Argyll & Bute
Argyll Caravan Park PA32 8XT (tel: 01499 302285)
South of Inveraray on A38, on shore of Loch Fyne.
Open early April to mid-October.

LOCHGILPHEAD
Argyll & Bute
Lochgilphead Caravan Site PA31 8NX (tel: 01546 602003)
On A83 close to town.
Open early April to mid-October..

TOUR 9
*LUSS Argyll & Bute
Camping & Caravanning Club Site G83 8NT (tel: 01436 860658 in season and 01203 694995)
¼ mile north of Luss village on A82 Glasgow – Fort William road. Very pretty site is just before village of Luss on shore of Loch Lomond.
Open end March to early November.

GLENDARUEL
Argyll & Bute
Glendaruel Caravan Park PA22 3AB (tel: 01369 820267)
Off A886.
Open early April to mid-October.

TOUR 10
LUSS Argyll & Bute
Camping & Caravanning Club Site G83 8NT (tel: 01436 860658 in season and 01203 694995)
Site is just north of village of Luss on shore of Loch Lomond.
Open end March to early November.

KIRRIEMUIR
Perthshire & Kinross
Drumshademuir Caravan Park Roundyhill DD8 1QT (tel: 01575 573284)
South of town on A928.
Open mid March to end October.

ABERFELDY
Perthshire & Kinross
Aberfeldy Caravan Park Dunkeld Road PH15 2AQ (tel: 01887 820662)
On east side of town, between main road and River Tay.
Open late March to late October.

CRIEFF Perthshire & Kinross
Crieff Holiday Village Turret Bank PH7 4JN (tel: 01764 653513)
Near Crieff, on A86 by river.
Open all year.

ABERFOYLE Stirling
Trossachs Holiday Park FK8 3SA (tel: 01877 382614)
Off A81, 3 miles south of Aberfoyle.
Open March to October.

TOUR 11
*CALLANDER Stirling
Callander Holiday Park Invertrossachs Road FK17 8HW (tel: 01877 330265)
From centre of Callander take A81 Glasgow road over bridge, then turn right in 200 yards towards Invertrossachs road, and site is 1/2 mile. No tents.
Open 15 March to October.

*AUCHTERARDER
Perthshire & Kinross
Auchterarder Caravan Site Nether Coul PH3 1ET (tel: 01764 663119)

Turn off A9 into Auchterarder, north of village take B8062 signposted Dunning. Turn left after 100 yards.
Open all year.

*EDINBURGH
City of Edinburgh
Mortonhall Caravan Park 38 Mortonhall Gate EH16 6TJ (tel: 0131 664 1533)
Located on south side of Edinburgh, within 20 minutes car ride of city centre, in the grounds of Mortonhall mansion. Follow A720 city bypass to junction with A702. Site signposted from here.
Open 28 March to October.

*AUCHENBOWIE Stirling
Auchenbowie Caravan & Camping Site FK7 8HE (tel: 01324 822141)
South of Stirling. Leave M9 at junction 9, turn right off A872 for 1/2 mile.
Open April to October.

TOUR 12
BIRNAM
Perthshire & Kinross
Erigmore House Holiday Park PH8 9XX (tel: 01350 727236)
Off A9 on B898, in grounds of Erigmore House. No tents.
Open March to October.

FORFAR Angus
Lochside Caravan Park
Forfar Loch Country Park DD8 1BT (tel: 01307 464201 and 468917)
Off ring road A94, close to loch.
Open late March to early October.

MONTROSE Angus
South Links Caravan Park
Traill Drive DD10 8EJ (tel: 01674 72026 and 72105)
From A92 follow signs for golf course.
Open late March to early October.

CARNOUSTIE Angus
Woodlands Caravan Park
Newton Road DD7 6HR (tel: 01241 854430 and 853246)
In the town, signposted from

A930. Open late March to early October.

INCHTURE
Perthshire & Kinross
Inchmarchtine Caravan Park & Nurseries Dundee Road PH14 9QQ (tel: 01821 670212 and 686251)
On A85. No tents.
Open March to October.

PERTH Perthshire & Kinross
Camping & Caravanning Club Site Scone Racecourse, Scone PH2 6BB (tel: 01738 552323 in season 01203 694995)
Next to Scone Racecourse, off A93.
Open end March to early November.

Cleeve Caravan Park
Glasgow Road PH2 0PH (tel: 01738 639521 and 474864)
Off A93, 2 miles west of Perth.
Open late March to late October.

TOUR 13
ST ANDREWS Fife
Craigtoun Meadows Holiday Park Mount Melville KY16 8PQ (tel: 01334 475959)
2 miles from town on Craigtoun road.
Open March to October.

Kinkell Braes Caravan Site
KY16 8PX (tel: 01334 474250)
On A917, 1 mile south of town.
Open 21 March to October.

ST MONANS Fife
St Monans Caravan Park
KY10 2DN (tel: 01333 730778 and 310185)
On A917 east of St Monans.
Open 21 March to October.

ELIE Fife
Shell Bay Caravan Park KY9 1HB (tel: 01333 330283)
11/2 miles northwest of Elie, off A917. Signed on unclassified road, close to beach.
Open 21 March to October.

LUNDIN LINKS Fife
Woodland Gardens Caravan & Camping Site Blindwell

Road KY8 5QG (tel: 01333 360319)
Off A917 coast road at Largo. Approach along narrow well-signed road.
Open March to October.

LETHAM FEUS Fife
Letham Feus Caravan Park
KY8 5NT (tel: 01333 350323)
On A916, 2 miles northeast of Kennoway.
Open April to September.

TOUR 14
NAIRN Highland
Nairn Lochloy Holiday Park
East Beach IV12 4PH (tel: 01667 453764)
On edge of town, by side of beach, off A96.
Open March to October.

Delnies Woods Caravan Park Delnies Wood IV12 5NX (tel: 01667 455281)
3 miles west of town, on A96.
Open Easter to October.

Spindrift Caravan & Camping Site Little Kildrummie IV12 5QU (tel: 01667 453992)
Off B9090 2 miles south of town.
Open April to October.

GRANTOWN-ON-SPEY
Highland
Grantown-on-Spey Caravan Park Seafield Avenue PH26 3JQ (tel: 01479 872474)
Near river 1/2 mile from town.
Open Easter to September.

*BOAT OF GARTEN
Highland
Campgrounds of Scotland
PH24 3BN (tel: 01479 831652)
In village close to River Spey and Loch Garten, off A95.
Open all year, but phone to check opening times over Christmas and New Year.

DAVIOT Highland
Auchnahillin Caravan Park
IV1 2XQ (tel: 01463 772286)
7 miles southeast of Inverness on B9154 off A9. Follow Daviot East signs.
Open Easter to October.

TOUR 15
LOSSIEMOUTH Moray
Silver Sands Leisure Park
Covesea, West Beach IV31 6SP
(tel: 01343 813262)
From Lossiemouth follow
B9040 2 miles west.
Open April to October.

FOCHABERS Moray
Burnside Caravan Site Keith
Road IV32 7PF (tel: 01343
820511 and 820362)
1/2 mile east of town off A96.
Open April to October.

TOUR 16
*CUMINESTOWN
Aberdeenshire
**East Balthangie Caravan
Park** East Balthangie AB53
7XY (tel: 01888 544261)
Site is in centre of tour, close to
Turriff. From Macduff follow
A98 east, then take B9027 to
New Byth, then unclassified
road signed New Deer to junc-
tion with farm road in 21/4
miles.
Open March to October

*KINTORE Aberdeenshire
Hillhead Caravan Park AB51
0YX (tel: 01467 632809)
South of Inverurie on A96.
Open 31 March to October.

*ALFORD Aberdeenshire
**Haugusthton House
Caravan** Site AB33 8NA (tel:
019755 62107)
In country park beside River
Don, 5 miles northwest of
Alford.
Open April to September.

TOUR 17
PITLOCHRY
Perthshire & Kinross
Faskally Caravan Park PH16
5LA (tel: 01796 472007)
11/2 miles north of Pitlochry on
B8019, by side of river.
Open 15 March to October.

BLAIR ATHOLL
Perthshire & Kinross
Blair Castle Caravan Park
PH18 5SR (tel: 01796 481263)
North of Pitlochry off A9
within the Atholl estate.
Open April to late October.

AVIEMORE Highland
Campgrounds of Scotland
Coylumbridge PH22 1QU (tel:
01479 810120)
Off A9, 11/2 miles east of
Aviemore on the Loch Morlich
road.
Open all year.

BOAT OF GARTEN
Highland
Campgrounds of Scotland
PH24 3BN (tel: 01479 831652)
In village close to River Spey
and Loch Garten, off A95.
Open all year.

BALLATER Aberdeenshire
**Anderson Road Caravan
Site** Anderson Road AB3 5QW
(tel: 013397 55727 in season
and 01569 762001)
From A93 turn west into
Victoria Road and left into
Braiche Road near town centre.
Site on river bank.
Open April to mid October.

TOUR 18
ABERDEEN Aberdeenshire
**Hazlehead Caravan Park &
Campsite** Groats Road AB1
8BL (tel: 01224 647647 and
321268 in season)
On western outskirts of city off
A944.
Open April to September.

STONEHAVEN
Aberdeenshire
**Queen Elizabeth Caravan
Site** AB3 2RD (tel: 01569
764041 in season and 762001)
Close to sea front at junction of
A90 and B979. No tents.
Open April to mid-October.

ABOYNE Aberdeenshire
Aboyne Loch Caravan Park
AB34 5BR (tel: 013398 86244)
1 mile east of town off A93
beside Aboyne Loch.
Open 31 March to October.

ALFORD Aberdeenshire
**Haugusthton House
Caravan Site** AB33 8NA (tel:
019755 62107)
In country park beside River
Don, 5 miles northwest of
Alford.
Open April to September.

TOUR 19
FORT WILLIAM Highland
**Glen Nevis Caravan &
Camping Park** Glen Nevis
PH33 6SX (tel: 01397 702191
and 705181)
2 miles off A82 on Glen Nevis
road. 21/2 miles from Fort
William.
Open 15 March to October.

CORPACH Highland
**Linnhe Caravan & Chalet
Park** PH33 7NL (tel: 01397
772376)
1 mile west of Corpach on A830
on shores of Loch Eil.
Open Easter to October.

**RESIPOLE (LOCH
SUNART)** Highland
Resipole Farm PH36 4HX
(tel: 01967 431617 and 431235)
On A861 between Salen and
Strontian.
Open April to September.

LOCHALINE Highland
**Fiunary Camping &
Caravanning Park** Morvern
PA34 5XX (tel: 01967 421225)
5 miles west on B849 by loch
side.
Open May to October.

TOUR 20
INVERGARRY Highland
Faichem Park Ardgarry Farm,
Faichem PH35 4HG (tel:
01809 501226)
Just off A87 1 mile west of
Invergarry.
Open 15 April to 15 October.

BALMACARA Highland
Reraig Caravan Site IV40
8DH (tel: 01599 566215)
On A87 at rear of Balmacara
Hotel.
Open mid April to September.

**Balmacara Woodland Camp
Site** IV40 8DN (tel: 01599
566321)
Off A87 signposted Balmacara
Square.
Open Easter to September.

APPLECROSS Highland
Applecross Campsite IV54
8ND (tel: 01520 744268 and
744284)

On unclassified road off A896, close to village.
Open Easter to October.

GAIRLOCH Highland
Sands Holiday Centre IV21 2DL (tel: 01445 712152)
3 miles west of Gairloch on B8021, close to beach.
Open 20 May to 10 September.

Gairloch Caravan & Camping Park Strath IV21 2BT (tel: 01505 614343 and 01445 712373)
Off A832 close to Loch Gairloch.
Open April to 15 October.

CANNICH Highland
Cannich Caravan & Camping Park IV4 7LN (tel: 01456 415364 and 415263)
On A831 200 yards south east of Cannich Bridge.
Open March to November.

TOUR 21
*****TAIN** Highland
Meikle Ferry Caravan & Camping Park IV19 1JX (tel: 01862 892292)
South of Bonar Bridge on A9 north of Tain.
Open all year.

SCOURIE Highland
Scourie Caravan & Camping Park Harbour Road IV27 4TG (tel: 01971 502060 and 502061)
Off A894 in centre of village, by beach.
Open Easter to September.

LAIRG Highland
Dunroamin Caravan Park Main Street IV27 4AR (tel: 01549 402447)
On A839 in village.
Open April to October.

TOUR 22
DORNOCH Highland
Grannie's Heilan Hame Holiday Park Embo IV25 3QD (tel: 01862 810383 and 810753)
North of Dornoch on unclassified road at Embo. On beach.
Open all year, but phone to check Christmas and New Year opening times..

REAY Highland
Dunvegan Euro Campsite KW14 7RQ (tel: 01847 81405)
Off A836 in centre of village.
Open May to October.

THURSO Highland
Thurso Caravan & Camping Site Smith Terrace, Scrabster Road KW14 7JY (tel: 01847 894545 and 01955 607772)
On west side of town, signposted off A882.
Open May to September.

JOHN O'GROATS Highland
John O'Groats Caravan Site KW1 4YS (tel: 01955 611329)
Off A9, close to passenger ferry.
Open April to October.

TOUR 23
DINGWALL Highland
Camping & Caravanning Club Site Jubilee Park IV15 9QZ (tel: 01349 862236 in season and 01203 694995)
Close to village centre.
Open end March to early November.

TAIN Highland
Meikle Ferry Caravan & Camping Park IV19 1JX (tel: 01862 892292)
South of Bonar Bridge on A9 North of Tain.
Open all year.

ROSEMARKIE Highland
Camping & Caravan Club Site IV10 8UW (tel: 01381 621117 in season and 01203 694995)
At Rosemarkie turn right onto promenade and site is in 100 yards.
Open end March to early September.

TOUR 24
*****BALMACARA** Highland
Reraig Caravan Site IV40 8DH (tel: 01599 566215)
On mainland.
On A87 at rear of Balmacara Hotel.
Open mid April to September.
Balmacara Woodland Camp Site IV40 8DN (tel: 01599 566321)
On mainland.

Off A87 signposted Balmacara Square.
Open Easter to September.

EDINBANE Highland
Loch Greshornish Caravan Site Borve, Arnisort IV51 9PS (tel: 01470 582230)
Off A850 on loch shore at Edinbane, approximately 12 miles from Portree.
Open April to October.

TOUR 25
LOCHALINE Highland
Fiunary Camping & Caravanning Park Morvern PA34 5XX (tel: 01967 421225)
On mainland before catching ferry to Mull.
5 miles west on B849 by loch side.
Open May to October.

OBAN Argyll & Bute
Oban Divers Caravan Park Glenshellach Road PA34 4QJ (tel: 01631 562755)
On mainland before catching ferry to Mull.
South of town.
Open 15 March to 15 November.

CRAIGNURE Argyll & Bute
Shieling Holidays PA65 6AY (tel: 01680 812496)
1 mile from ferry landing at water's edge.
Open April to October.
Balmacara Woodland Camp Site IV40 8DN (tel: 01599 566321)
On mainland.
Off A87 signposted Balmacara Square.
Open Easter to September.

EDINBANE Highland
Loch Greshornish Caravan Site Borve, Arnisort IV51 9PS (tel: 01470 582230)
Off A850 on loch shore at Edinbane, approximately 12 miles from Portree.
Open April to October.

INDEX

Index

The Automobile Association
wishes to thank the following libraries and photographers for their assistance
in the preparation of this book.

IMAGE BANK front cover top picture (R. Lockyer)
INTERNATIONAL PHOTOBANK 124
PICTURES COLOUR LIBRARY 4
POWERSTOCK PHOTO LIBRARY front cover main picture
SPECTRUM COLOUR LIBRARY 5, 131

The remaining photographs are held in the Association's own photo library (AA PHOTO LIBRARY) and were taken by
the following photographers:
M ALEXANDER 6, 12, 22, 30B, 36B, 40, 41, 42, 44B, 45, 46A, 47, 50A, 50B, 76B; A BAKER 67A, 82; J BEAZLEY 10, 16, 17,
19, 20, 24/5, 26A, 26B, 30A, 42/3, 46B, 51, 61A, 61B, 77, 87B, 88, 109, 128; J CARNIE 7, 33, 56B, 62/3, 64, 67B, 71B, 78, 90,
104, 107B, 120, 212A, 121B, 144; D CORRANCE inside flap, 34, 38, 65, 75A, 76A, 118; S DAY back cover (a), 52, 57B, 58,
59A, 66, 68, 70, 72, 73, A, 73B, 75B, 79, 83B, 85, 86, 105A, 119A, 119B, 122; E ELLINGTON 87A, 93, 94/5, 97, 98A, 99,
103A, 110, 113, 115, 125, 132/3, 136B, 139A, 139B, 147A, 148, 154; R ELLIOTT 48, 53, 117A, 123, 126/7; D FORSS 55A,
55B, 157; S GIBSON PHOTOGRAPHY 14, 28, 29, 60; A GREELEY 150B; D HARDLEY 57A, 116; J HENDERSON 89,
106A, 107A, 111B, 114B, 132, 134A, 140, 142, 143, 150A, 151, 153; C LEES 25, 35, 44A; S & O MATTHEWS 18/9;
K PATTERSON back cover (B and C), 8, 11, 21, 32, 37, 49A, 49B, 56A, 62, 69, 81, 84, 111A, 112, 130B, 145A, 145B;
P SHARPE 9, 13, 23, 31, 59B, 92; M TAYLOR 36A, 74, 83A, 101B, 103B, 130A, 134B, 136A, 138, 146, 147B; R WEIR 80, 91,
96/7, 100, 101A, 102, 105B, 108, 112/3, 114A, 135, 137, 141, 149, 152, 155A, 156; H WILLIAMS 27, 39, 106B.

Contributors
Verifier: Emma Stanford   **Copy editor:** Dilys Jones   **Indexer:** Marie Lorimer